To – Doris

UWHARRIE BIZARRES

Colorful Characters from
America's Oldest Mountains

my very best wishes!

FRED T. MORGAN

Fred T. Morgan

12-8-07

BANDIT
BOOKS

Winston-Salem, North Carolina

Copyright © 2007 by Fred T. Morgan
All rights reserved
Printed in the United States of America

Library of Congress Control Number 2007930876
ISBN 978-1-878177-17-9

Bandit Books, Inc.
P.O. Box 11721
Winston-Salem, NC 27116-1721
(336) 785-7417

Distributed by John F. Blair, Publisher
(800) 222-9796
www.blairpub.com

Photographs on pages 26, 46, 78, 90, 112, 186, 195, and
201 courtesy of Brooks Barnhardt

All other photographs from Morgan Family Archives

CONTENTS

Introduction   1

The Hermit   9

The Tombstone Man   19

The Shotgun Man   27

Uncle Lucian's Light   33

The Smooth Stone Man   41

Real Special Vigg-a   47

The Tree Painter   53

The Man Who Made Sunshine   59

The Shoo Fly Man   67

Old Time Bill Collector   73

The Man Who Jerked   79

The Disciplinarian   87

Lanky Dan The Shelter Man   91

Aunt Hattie   97

The One-Story Man   103

Ol' Bullet   113

The Perpetual Motion Man   121

Jess Greene The Story Machine   125

The Buzzard Man   137

Miracle at 100 MPH   143

This Ol' House   151

The Voice   159

Lady in the Library   171

Ol' Tobe's Tomfoolery   179

The Strange Interlude   187

Fifty Dollars   197

ACKNOWLEDGMENT

Scores of people have helped me in various ways in my research and writing during the past half century. Naming all of them is impossible. Many have passed on. Many others are irretrievably lost in the limbo. To all of these I give a sincere salute of acknowledgment and gratitude.

Randomly listed below, in addition to my family members and close friends, are individuals who have helped me in countless ways. My heartfelt thanks and appreciation goes to each and every one:

John B. Harris, George B. Weaver, John F. Blair, Jerry Bledsoe, Barry McGee, Carolyn Sakowski, Dick and Margie Jarrett, Brooks and Jane Barnhardt, Henry and Bonnie Springer, Heather Ross Miller, Bridget Huckabee, Brenda S. Cox, Stephanie D. Brown, Martha L. Rogers, Anabel Speight, Bill Turner, LaRue H. Deese, Charlie McSwain, Floyd A. Griffin, Ray A. Griffin, Fred T. Adams, Opal W. Biles, Virginia S. Foglia, Betty P. Turner, Leon D. Parker, Rex A. Maynor, Robert Fisher, Nettie Loflin, Gerald and Sue Morgan, Richard Bunn, Louise Leonard Bowman, John Glenn Tucker, Troy Clayel Springer, Luedith W. Underwood, Peggy K. Morton, Dock Watson, Daniel Kirk, Clyde E. B. Bernhardt, Vivian V. Harris, J. Wallace Ivy, Lacy L. Cranford, Myra Slate, Brooks Wilson, Jim Wicker, Rose Post, Henry King, David Deese, Henry E. Farmer, Lucy Snuggs, Pricilla Clark, Adam G. Almond, Pam Holbrook, Lori Downing and Rick Jarrett.

While the identity of the two women with the ox-drawn logging wagon has not been ascertained, this picture is believed to have been made in Stanly County in the early 1900s.

INTRODUCTION

When I started roaming central North Carolina's Uwharrie Mountains shortly after World War II in the late 1940s, I had no idea I was engaging in a form of folklore research. The term had never occurred to me. It would not have registered had someone told me that's what I was doing. Only many years later did the term formalize itself in my consciousness and vocabulary. I wrote my first book the same way; I went ahead and did it without knowing how. My early research followed the same format. The technique I used produced satisfying results. Why try to academically fix the unbroken naturalness?

Dignity—human dignity—is a word I do understand and I used it to enormous advantage then and for the rest of my productive life, although this usage, and the psychology involved, sprang forth purely from instinct.

Reflecting on it now, I'm glad I didn't use formality in my approach to the country people I talked to back then. Most of them would have been spooked into some form of hostility and skepticism. Eyes would have narrowed. Frowns developed. Doors would've slammed. Heads would have shook in dismissal. Fertile ground would have become barren in my quest. I learned that these people needed a little extra time to mull over and get used to an idea—even a simple idea or suggestion as mine was. Formality doesn't give them enough mulling time. Informality does. I always had plenty of time in this pursuit.

In my old pickup, I kept a pair of coveralls, boots, brogans, straw hat, gloves and a few basic working tools. My upbringing had prepared me for hands-on participation in all kinds of rural, farm, and handyman activity. I enjoyed wholesome work. No matter the season, most farm families were always busy when I stopped to visit. All of them, all of the time—the adults, children, male, female, young and old—they were always busy in the field or woods with some chore around the barnyard, homestead or pastures. I pitched in and helped, no matter what they were doing.

My introduction didn't vary much. "My name's Morgan. I'm from Albemarle. I'm collecting stories about the old days. After we work a while, I would like to hear any old scary stories you've heard about haunted houses, ghosts, strange lights and noises, old witch women... you know... even those strange people who can talk out fire and cure the thrash and make warts go away... but... let me help you... let's work a while first."

The message soaked in. The key part of it was "... after we work a while...let's work a while first." When a lull came in the work—a mid-morning or mid-afternoon break, dinnertime, suppertime, a breakdown, a rainstorm, or darkness—then we'd talk. I had helped them, so they felt some obligation to reciprocate, to help me. And they always did. I absorbed a vast amount of folklore material this way, practically all of it unrecorded except for storage in my memory.

Here is where the dignity came in. No matter how menial the task, I surrounded it with important priority, giving it my unswerving interest and attention to detail, including all the individuals involved. I praised their performance. I asked questions. I found an opportunity to try my hand at the work. Many times I pretended ineptness in order to be coaxed and informed. Always, these people, their work and craftsmanship were superior. I remained the underdog, the learner, the eager neophyte who appreciated all their efforts. Cooperation flourishes in such an atmosphere. As we labored together, they had ample time to think about what I wanted, why I was there, why I had stopped to visit. I put forth genuine, strong-back labor for them with no thought of monetary recompense. At the proper time they responded. The old barter system at work.

On each foray into the Uwharries, I traveled a different road into a new community, picking the more remote and backwoodsy areas. More than half the time, I never got to the dwelling house. I spotted the family members at work, so I approached them at the work site. Almost any activity around a rural farmstead can use an extra helping hand.

Over the years, I participated in scores of chores, just about every type of rural living/farm work imaginable. Such as: plowing behind a team of mules, pulling fodder, well digging, clearing new ground, dynamiting stumps, castrating calves, seining fish ponds, chopping and picking cotton, thinning and pulling com, hauling hay, tying and shocking bundles of wheat, wheat threshing, cribbing ear com after a com shucking, cutting firewood with a crosscut saw, hog killing, kraut making, green bean pickling, crosstie cutting, nailing tin on a barn roof, cleaning out stables, re-locating the outhouse, building fences, hand-milking a cow, herb gathering, offbearing heavy slabs and green lumber at a sawmill, digging a hole to bury a dead mule, pumping the forge bellows at the blacksmith shop, turning the grindstone for sharpening tools, chair bottoming, drying fruit in the sun, channeling spring water into the house, churning butter, hiving bees, hilling potatoes, building retaining walls out of natural rock, terracing hillside fields by hand and by natural eyesight, making homemade soap and brooms, tanning hides for leather, stirring binned wheat, birthing calves and foals, molasses making, cider making, re-building a fallen down native stone chimney, clipping chicken wings, learning the best way to steal chickens, building a wooden wagon body, re-lining the brakes on a two-horse wagon, and patching holes in burlap bags.

Moonshining would factor in among the countless other activities not listed.

Through it all, I enjoyed every minute of it. As a willing worker, I developed an inimitable camaraderie with the people I worked with, leading to some longtime friendships. It never occurred to me *not* to participate in these work sessions. My parents taught me the work ethic from boyhood: if there's work to be done, get on with it, go the extra mile. This practice found universal acceptance in the Uwharries.

Twenty years must have passed before I learned that I was, indeed, engaging in authentic, bona fide folklore research. But...I was going about it all wrong. I talked to a few other folklorists during this period. None of them shared my enthusiasm for direct hands-on involvement in the routine work of these native people. Nor did I volunteer any elaboration on my technique. All they wanted to do was talk, ask questions and record responses, if any. Much too formal for me; too inhumane. I don't blame the natives for not responding. I wouldn't have, either. We were after the same thing, essentially, to record and preserve a fast-vanishing segment of colorful Americana. The formalizers wanted quick access, quick responses, quick departures, so they could use laboratory scrutiny to analyze and catalogue their gleanings. All I wanted was stories. Rarely did I possess or use any mechanical recording device. But I maximized a trained memory.

Occasionally, a formalized folklore researcher would complain to me: "They won't talk to me. I can't get 'em to open up. When I bring out that microphone, they recoil, they clam up, they're too busy, they tell me to come back later or try the next family on over the road. How do you do it?"

Never one to share all my secrets, I would answer non-committally and say something like: "I just spend a little more time working with them."

Two things happened to lessen my research safaris into the Uwharries. Age slowed me down a bit. But, mainly, it was the thinning out of elderly people who knew much about the old days. Some visits I could knock on doors and go to work-sites for hours, for half a day, without finding any older people with yarns to tell. Rapidly, this older generation began fading away—and with it went the material I sought. Their descendants, the younger people, had little interest in preserving what their forebears loved to talk about. Sadly, scores of these human reservoirs of choice Uwharrie folklore passed on before I had a chance to talk with them. Gone beyond any recall. Now it is difficult to find a

senior native Uwharrian with any new folklore. No use even asking the young ones. Modernity has practically wiped out this
ghostly folklore potential and left little in its place appealing to
me.

A satisfying sideline developed along with my ghost story
collecting.

I began to encounter a series of colorful characters–oddball individuals, eccentrics, deviant people, many with artistic
skills and temperaments to match. I could call them freaks or
weirdos, even bizarre, but I prefer to categorize them as colorful
characters. Since I probably fall into this category myself, I generated an intense affinity for these special people. This attraction
proved mutual, for, more and more, I felt drawn, directed to
these individuals spontaneously, then captivated by them. Instinct played a crucial role in most of these confrontations.
Though they occurred in the late 1940s, through the 1950s and
into the 1960s, these experiences embedded themselves into my
memory with such clarity they could have happened last week.
All these people are long gone now. No vestige remains of them
or their unique contributions. Nor could I ever find my way
back to the original locations where these encounters took place.

Always, I will ponder this question: what strange combi-
nation of circumstances and mystical synchronization placed
these people into my pathway? It's part of the Uwharrie
allurement.

I fondly hope this book, together with my earlier
Uwharrie books, will make a valid contribution toward the pres-
ervation of an inimitable lifestyle and cultural canvas centered so

vividly here in this unique frontier on our great American continent.

Come with me now—let's meet, mingle and enjoy my bizarres from my safaris into **my** Uwharries.

Regarded as the last genuine hermit in the area, Carlton H. Seeley lived for decades in this shack in the Uwharrie remoteness. He froze to death in nine-degree weather outside the shack during the Christmas holiday period in 1972.

THE HERMIT

It took half a day to find the whereabouts of the Hermit, the man with an epochal message for mankind, which he never got to deliver. But I'm glad I persisted, for he remains one of the more bizarre of the Uwharrie bizarres I encountered.

"Take this old dirt road down through the woods," my informer said. "You'll see a big rock beside the road. Half as big as your pickup. You can pull off and park there. You'll see a trail into the woods. Follow it."

Terse. Laconic. He had already eyed me pretty carefully, convinced I meant no harm to anyone. Uwharrians are like that.

But in no remote way did he prepare me for what I encountered in the next few minutes after I parked.

I slung my camera over my shoulder, locked my truck and hit the trail. Immediately, the woods thickened. The fully leaved foliage whispered a bit ominously. An invisible scampering noise paced me in the bushes off the trail. Crows cawed in the canopy way overhead. Somehow, the woods, along with the oppressive heat, closed in around me like prison walls which you can't see, but you know are there. My steps slowed as apprehension gripped me, tickling the hairs on my neck and accelerating my heartbeat. I stopped. My uneasiness increased. Here I was alone in the isolation of the big woods, not knowing who or what awaited me in the next moment, in the next step or two. Should I abandon this mission? Should I leave and come back later with another person or two with me for moral support?

My feet solved my indecision. Automatically, they took me forward a few paces.

Then I saw it!

Through the trees, almost magically, appeared a decrepit, weather-blackened shack, impressive in its decadence. A rusty screen door listed over two huge slate slabs serving as a stoop. Tattered screens partially covered a window on either side of the door, some of the glass panes cracked and broken, stuffed with newspaper and rags. Green moss and a fern or two grew out of the debris around the edge of the roof. I could almost smell the mustiness coming from the inside.

I rapped on the side of the old door. No response. I rapped louder. No response. "Hello-oo, anybody home?" I half yelled. Silence.

"Leave–get outta here," my logical mind told me.

But I resisted. Maybe the occupant was around back, so I decided to check out the backside of the shack. I started around the corner. Right then and there, I experienced one of the greatest shocks of my life.

We met at the corner, each recoiling and staggering. We did more than meet; we collided. Head-on. Eyeball to eyeball. My camera strap slid off my shoulder and the camera case thudded to the ground at my feet. My mouth flew open. My eyes bulged. I uttered some staccato syllables in complete shock. For a few long seconds, my vocal chords produced only gibberish.

He stood there, enjoying my reaction, amusement on his face, at least the tiny portion of his face visible. Dirty gray hair covered practically all his face and head. Long, knotty tangles of gray hair flared around his neck, and spilled over across his forehead to merge with a wiry mustache and a beard, which appeared to grow up as well as down, the downward portion reaching his waist. Birds could nest in that twisty mass of gray, maybe even a squirrel. Faded blue eyes gleamed like beacons amid that ghostliness of gray. The tip of his nose protruded. When he spoke, a line of murkiness marked the location of his mouth. He wore tattered overalls, patched again and again at the knees. Scrawny arms poured out of a sleeveless shirt, ending in hands so crusty they looked like small stumps blackened by a new ground fire.

He bent and picked up my camera and handed it to me.

"Welcome to my humble abode," he gestured. "Who sent you to see me?"

His distinct voice sounded strangely sophisticated in this primitive setting. "A neighbor of yours back over the road told me how to find you," I answered, relieved at his apparent friendliness.

He nodded.

For the next two-three hours, I asked dozens of questions. He not only answered, but discoursed and sermonized, sometimes in grandiose fashion. He talked with the shrewdness of a politician, the erudition of a university professor, the emotionalism of a preacher, the vision of a philosopher, the passion of an activist.

He talked about everything and then some. Whatever subject I mentioned, he knew lots more about it than I did. He knew all the big names in all the big fields, all the progressive advancement in science, medicine, industry, religion, business, government, and technology. I tried to think of names of obscure celebrities, exotic foreign locations, difficult Biblical passages, geographic anomalies, famous quotations, and historical trivia. Rarely did I mention anything he could not expand upon. He knew American and European history and could quote dates and highlights. Among his favorite writers were Shakespeare and Mark Twain, from whom he could quote extensively. The more I asked him, the more intense and voluminous became his replies, as he relished this opportunity to talk, talk, talk. His skinny arms, loose flab trembling, gestured emphatically to emphasize his points.

Finally, mentally exhausted, I told him I had to leave, but I wanted to see the inside of his shack first. He led me to the door and motioned me inside.

Only one person could stand just inside the door. Miscellaneous furnishings and junk, dusty and cobwebby, jammed the interior lengthwise and top to bottom. A pathway of sorts, strewn with moldy stacks of newspapers and magazines, led toward a corner bed rumpled with smelly covers. My eyes and mind quickly took in shelves full of books, one set of encyclopedia among them; a rusty wood burning stove, cardboard boxes stuffed with reading material, a dresser, table, chest and the end of an old organ, all practically hidden by junk; buckets, a kerosene lamp, candles, odd clothing and bedding, musical instruments, a framed picture or two on the wall flanking a wide global map. I spotted a wasp nest in one corner of the ceiling. A mouse squeaked at me and ran. A wren flew out a hole in the window. The darkness made me seek fresh air.

Next, he guided me to another smaller shack, one hundred feet or so away, which he identified as his kitchen and dining room. It contained a wood burning cook stove, a rickety wooden table, a bench and various cooking utensils strewn about and hanging from nails. A galvanized bucket half full of water sat on the edge of a smaller table, the handle of a gourd dipper protruding from it. This is where he cooked and ate the vegetables he grew in a nearby hand spaded organic garden. The water came from a natural spring. Fruit, berries, nuts, fish, an occasional trapped rabbit and squirrel rounded out his diet.

"Look!" he said.

He bent low, straight-legged, and touched his finger to the ground. He jumped and caught a limb and pulled his chin over it twice.

"No creaky bones," he said. "No straining muscles."

He made me guess his age and I guessed seventy. "Add fifteen more years," he said.

Once more at the shack, he led me around back. He directed my attention to an uneven break in a stack of firewood and slabs. A big round headlamp, glass rim intact, became visible amid the firewood. He caressed the curved end of a front fender nearby. All the rest of the vehicle—top, bottom, and inside—was covered with rotting firewood.

"That's what I drove down here from up Nauth," he said, patting the fender. "My '28 T-Model."

"And this is how you preserved it," I mused. He nodded.

I photographed him in several locations around the shack and asked him if I could write a story about him for a newspaper or magazine.

He shook his head. "Time's not right. I have an important message to share with mankind...but I gotta wait till the time's right...till I get the right signal. Then I'll share it...then you can write about me."

I tried to get a clue about the nature of this vital message, but he evaded every question. Was it Biblical? Divine? Philosophical? Supremely inspired? Revolutionary? Why was he chosen, in these humble surroundings, as the channel through which this information would be released?

"It's for humanity," he said, "but the time's not right."

I gave him my name, address and phone number and told him to call me, night or day, when the time was right. He said he would contact me.

Late in the day, I left reluctantly, my mind raging with quotes and images of this mysterious hermit of the Uwharries. The longer I drove away from his shack, the more dreamlike the experience became. Reality returned next day when my processed film and black and white prints created a sensation in and around the darkroom. My pictures of the hermit have since taken on classic overtones.

During the next year or so, I visited the hermit at least twice more, each time trying to learn more about his message for mankind and trying to gain permission to print a story about him. Adamantly, he refused. The time wasn't right. He would contact me.

But I did learn a lot more about him.

His name was Carlton H. Seeley, a native of Virginia. He worked in the automotive industry in the Detroit area where he developed a health problem. His doctor advised him to come south to live. On his way to Arkansas, his old car broke down, stranding him here in the Uwharries. Local residents were so kind in helping him, he fell in love with the people and the environment and decided this was far enough south. He paid $100 for twenty-eight acres in the wilds and, with some help from neighbors, began building his shack over and around his disabled Model-T.

Slowly, he merged with the community, proving his acceptability. He worked part-time for nearby farmers, part-time at the slate mine and other odd jobs. He caught rides to town or the nearest store for necessities. Mostly he just enjoyed the isolation of the big woods and his simple lifestyle. He tamed some small animals and claimed he could communicate with them. He composed original songs and sang to the creatures around him. Likewise, he lectured to his animal friends and preached sermons to them. Approaching visitors could hear him singing and discoursing to an audience they, themselves, could not see. He told me he was so spiritually attuned that he could obtain help and enlightenment almost immediately from otherworld entities. The more mysterious the subject under discussion, the better he liked it. The supernatural fascinated him.

How did he obtain all this knowledge?

"Reading," he said.

Neighbors and friends recycled their reading material to him, all of which he devoured. His retention and memory amazed me. If I questioned a fact or statement, he could quote the source, the name of the publication, the date, page number and headline. Also, he listened to news on a battery-powered radio.

"Meditating, too," he added.

Quiet, prolonged meditation produced excellent results for him. He said he always found enlightenment and enrichment in meditation and contemplation, supplemented by his visualization techniques. Knowledge is out there all around us all the time, just waiting for us to seize and utilize it, he said.

"I can close my eyes and concentrate a moment and get any answer I want anytime," he said. He tapped his head again. "The human mind is unlimited...it can do anything."

I pressed him for more clues about his mega-message for mankind.

He shook his head. "Time's not right. The signal's coming. Gotta wait for the signal. Synchronization. Everybody's gotta be ready and listening. I'll know instantly. I'll let you know. I'll be in touch. I'll contact you when the time's right."

Time ran out for Mr. Seeley, the hermit, during the Christmas holidays of 1972. Neighbors found him frozen to death on the snowy ground outside the door of his shack. Officials believed he came outside, perhaps to get firewood for his heater, suffered a sudden attack and died quickly. Marks in the snow showed how he struggled in vain to get the few feet back inside. The temperature that night dropped to nine degrees.

A cousin in Virginia claimed the body and took it back there for burial. All the hermit's worldly possessions, including the shack's contents and the old car, were auctioned at a sale attracting hundreds of people, some paying exorbitant prices for nondescript items. A few people likened attendance at this sale to a memorial service or final tribute to this man of the wilds who had intrigued so many.

Today, I can drive the road near his former shack location and feel his mysticism creeping into me and reviving my memory of him. Foremost in these memories is the promise he made to contact me when the time was right for his revelation to mankind.

Nothing more has surfaced about the nature of this message, though speculation has been rife about its cataclysmic potential.

Decades have passed with no indication that Mr. Seeley is ready to communicate from the 'other side'. Of course, time is of no consequence in the spiritual realm. And, assuredly, it is from the spiritual world that this contact must come. When it comes, I'll do all I can to circulate it the way he intended.

Meantime, I'm ready and waiting.

THE TOMBSTONE MAN

I had praised his artwork so enthusiastically, the tombstone man made me an offer:

"Stick around a little while longer and I"ll make one just for you," he said. "While you wait–give it to you, to boot."

An offer almost irresistible. Impulsively, I said, "No thanks."

He looked surprised, grinning. Grinning trademarked this man.

Foolishly, I had turned down an offer for an original, hand-tooled, customized native stone marker for the head of my grave.

In vigorous good health, hyperactive and brimming with optimism, I had scarcely ever thought about death and dying, never to the point where I would actually need a grave and a headstone; I found it repulsive even to think about dying and grave marking in a personal way. That was for other people, older people, not me.

Now, fifty years later, I keep reprimanding myself for not having accepted his offer. Death and dying do cross my mind, though I never dwell on it. The significance of adequate grave marking has registered with me. If I possessed one of the Tombstone Man's customized originals today, I would cherish it as a valuable family heirloom and leave clear instructions for its use and placement at the proper time.

It's too late now. I'll never have another chance like that. So, all that's left is memories, but thanks for the memories....

Instinct introduced me to the Tombstone Man. Rounding a curve on this old country road I stopped and looked at something unusual. A private drive, hardly noticeable, led off around a hill and into some trees. Stacks of something dark dotted the trees. I moved closer.

When I stopped at the little vine-covered shop resembling a blacksmith shop, a rasping noise spilled out the open door. But the operator had already seen me. He stopped grinding and came outside, brushing powdery dust off his coveralls. He pushed back a cap, removed goggles from his eyes and extended his hand.

"They call me the Tombstone Man," he said, grinning and waving his hand around to let the premises confirm his claim. "You need a grave marker? I feel so good today that I'll sell you one at a discount, even two."

I shook my head, grinning, too, at the irony of such a happy man engrossed in a death-related business.

"Don't need a marker," I said. "But I do need to know what you do with all those mounds of gray slate stacked around here?"

So, he began telling me.

"Well, it started like this. There's a natural slate quarry on the creek back over here. Oodles of it. Never run out. I squirrel hunted a lot as a boy. One day I walked along the creek under that slate bank with my .22 rifle. Just a boy, not even in my teens yet. A piece of slate fell off that bank and landed right in front of me. It was about the proper size and shape and thickness for a regular marker. Rough, though. Needed finishing up. But let me tell you what happened to it.

"When it fell, it landed on the sharp edgy point of a big round rock and sorta skidded around. I lugged it up and turned it over. Right there under the top edge was the prettiest rainbow scratch you ever saw. That collision and sliding created that rainbow scratched into that slab-o'slate. Right at the right place, too. Almost perfect. I kneeled down and examined it close. Couldn't hardly shape a better rainbow even today."

"Well, right then something else happened, significant. The sun busted out from behind a cloud and shined down on me and that rock so bright...so bright that it was almost dazzling. I was amazed. I looked up at the sun Then I looked at the way it lit up that slate and made that scratched rainbow stand out so clear. I dropped my .22. If a dozen squirrels had come outta the trees, I wouldn't-a shot at nary a one. I couldn't do anything but hug that slab-o' slate that I believe God put a rainbow on. Just for me.

"A divine revelation from God? Yeah. Just for me, too. That bright sunshine shafting down on me. All white and light and pure and dazzling. Yeah. It was a call. I felt thrilled, inspired. Like God was directing me. He and I knowed what for. He wanted me to make pretty grave markers. He showed me how to get started. He helped me make the first one. I been—He's been helping me make them ever since. And He told me to be happy while I was doing it, because I was doing it to help other people."

I interrupted his whistling with a question.

"You do more than just the rainbow design, don't you?"

Motioning me to follow, he showed me around.

Random stacks of grave markers decorated the inside and outside of the shop. All were the approximate same length, width and thickness. Many were finished on the top edge with a variety of designs—rounded, shouldered, pointed, rainbows, ribbed, towered, scalloped, serrated. Below the top edge, he etched designs of all sorts—a dove, olive branch, praying hands, rising sun, open Bible, angels, a cross, the all-seeing eye, a flag, the beloved head of Christ. Vacant space for names and dates followed. A short epitaph could go at the bottom.

"Most people pick one from my stock," he said. "Saves time. Then I just etch in the names and dates."

Do people pay him for the markers?

"Some give me a few dollars, some don't," he said. "Others leave some produce, eggs, chickens, game, a hunk of cured meat, a quilt, a baked cake or pie. They bring me a sack of flour or a bag of meal, a load of firewood, help me patch my roof, give me a ride to town when I need to go, things like that. They look after me. They don't let me suffer."

He had no family, lived alone, absorbed with grave marker production every day of his life.

"I install 'em too, if they ask me to," he said. "Takes a lot of time, but I don't charge anything extra. Death and burying is always a bad time for the family. I try to turn it into a good time. I'm always a-whistlin' and a-hummin' while I work."

He accomplished most of his work with simple hand tools, most improvised, some outright inventions, clever ones, too. He commented on that.

"I know I couldn't-a done it by myself without special tools and arrangements. But I didn't sweat about it. Just kept going. Kept tinkering. An idea would come to me on how to solve it. And it worked. When I needed something special, it always turned up. Still does. I can cut and saw, chisel and shape, rasp and sand and buff, etch and sketch, glaze and engrave. I've learned how to make the heavy light and the hard easy. Not all by myself, though, couldn't do it without Him."

In full swing, everything gets to humming in the old shack. I listened and marveled. Every clang, wham, crack, yaw, rasp, whine, scratch, squeak and rustle of the tools and equipment, every creak, crack, groan and moan, rattle and quiver of the shack; all merged harmoniously with the unmistakable master craftsman and his melody divine.

Rarely had I seen such one-man harmony with nature.

"Nobody ever bothers me much unless they need a marker," he said. "They always know they can get a marker here anytime they want it."

He said no one ever hung around and watched his actual work. They just wrote down the names and dates for him, then returned later for the finished marker. A lot of his finished work occurred at night. No one ever assisted him in the work, either, that is no one physical.

This puzzled a lot of people. How did he produce such beautiful artistic work, perfectly proportioned and executed, without any modern, sophisticated equipment?

The Tombstone Man's turnover speed became amazing, too. In an emergency, you could leave the specifications with him in the morning and pick up the finished work in the afternoon of the same day. Even starting from scratch with a blank piece of raw slate, he could have a completed marker ready for you the second day.

Folks said his efficiency increased along with his age.

Though busy, he always had plenty of leisure time when anyone visited his shop or needed his services.

What kind of marker was he preparing for himself?

He showed me.

From a shelf under a bench, he pulled a marker, dusted it and stood it upright for me to see. Under the rounded top, a perfect rainbow arched symmetrical lines to both edges. Sun-light sent shafts of light on it from above. Angels floated under it. Or was one of those angels in the shape of the Tombstone Man? There were no dates down in the middle space, just the words: THE TOMBSTONE MAN. Engraved in the epitaph space at the bottom were the words: He Keeps Me Singing.

He told me, "I don't know when I was born. I don't know when I'll die. I don't know where I'll be buried. I just leave that up to the neighbors and the Good Lord."

Years later, I made some inquires, but didn't learn anything. Nobody knew when he died, how he died or where he was buried. Nor did anyone know what happened to his shop and stock.

It just wasn't there anymore.

THE SHOTGUN MAN

The old dirt road grew rougher and more narrow as I navigated through an isolated section of the Uwharries where I had never been before. Erosion had left a series of shallow gullies across the road bed which my battered pickup slithered into and climbed out of. A small stream gurgled lazily across the road. Limbs and bushes threatened to swipe my vehicle from either side. I hadn't passed a dwelling house in at least a mile. Yet, there were signs of recent traffic on the road—not much traffic, but a little. Maybe, just maybe, the old road would connect with a better road and enable me to find my way out to some civilization again.

As I emerged from a patch of woods, I looked across the clearing and saw a figure materialize from the bushes and stand in the middle of the road.

Apprehension gripped me.

Slowly, I moved closer and stopped within a few feet of the figure. My apprehension increased as I took in more detail.

An old farmer, wearing dirty, patched overalls and a soiled blue work shirt, stood there glowering at me. I could feel the intensity of his faded blue eyes, slightly glazed, boring into me. A ragged straw hat pressed down on his gray hair, locks of which were sweat-plastered to his forehead. A week's whiskers covered his face. Dried tobacco juice dribbled from the corners of his mouth. The overall galluses pinned down the collars of his shirt. He stood there straight and stiff as if a military boot camp

27

sergeant had ordered him to attention.

My throat tightened in alarm now as another detail registered on me.

His gnarled hands gripped a double-barreled shotgun right in front of him. The barrel angled upward, the fingers of his right hand played around the trigger guard.

I started to get out, but he came around and stood, bent over a little, by the open window of my truck door, the menacing gun still clutched tightly against his middle. He scrutinized the truck and me carefully.

"Stranger here, ain't ya?"

"Yes, Sir, I've never been here before," I said.

His twangy voice sounded halfway between a grunt and a growl.

"What's yer business?"

"I'm doing folklore research," I said. "I drive out these old country roads and talk to people about the old days."

His eyes narrowed. Half a scowl clouded his face as if he didn't believe a word I said. He muttered unintelligibly.

"This here's private property, ya know," he growled.

I nodded.

"State road ended way back over yonder."

I didn't say anything.

"Private property means you're trespassing," he said, re-gripping his gun for emphasis. "You know yer a trespasser, don't ye?"

"Yes, Sir, I guess I am," I said. "But I didn't see any signs. I was hoping this old road would connect with a better road so I could find my way outta here."

"Naw, it just deadends on down here a ways."

His hand left the gun long enough to swat a gnat.

"Trespassers get shot at sometimes, ya know," he leered.

I didn't say anything. I was too scared to say anything.

"You ever been shot at?"

"No, Sir", I quavered. But then I added: "Well, I was in World War II, so I guess I do remember some bullets whizzing over my head."

He nodded, his eyes half closed, like he could identify with that; like he could remember bullets whistling past his head.

"You don't want to be shot at anymore, do ya?"

"No, Sir, I don't. I sure don't want to be shot at anymore."

He looked at me closely, studying my face. Not once did his hands leave that shotgun.

My mind raced. Was he toying with me? Trying to make me terrorize myself by visualizing horrible penalties and punishment he intended to inflict on me for trespassing on private property? Stark images flooded my consciousness. Would I be mugged? Knocked down, kicked and stomped? Brutalized? My legs shot out from under me as I tried to run? My truck vandalized?

Finally, he turned and spat a big slug of tobacco juice into the bushes, turning back and swiping his mouth on his sleeve.

"Wal, I reckon there's only one thing to do," he said gruffly. His hands tightened noticeably on the shotgun.

I tensed, my heart skipped beat or two. Should I try to shove the old man backward into the bushes and then make a run for it?

"Yep, there's only one way to handle this sit-u-ation," he said firmly. His cold eyes, glowered contemptuously.

Slowly, methodically, inches from my eyes, he broke open the breech part of the shotgun, exposing the shiny ends of the two loaded shells. He took out each shell, examined it and replaced it. He snapped the breech shut with an ominous clack.

My hand tensed on the door handle. Should I try kicking the door open hard enough to knock the old man back into the briar patch and disorient him while I cranked up and blasted backward outta there?

He sensed my desperation.

"I wouldn't try anything foolish, like trying to escape," he said. "We're not through with you yet."

He stepped back and his eyes swept over my old truck for an instant.

"Nice old pickup you got here. We can sell it for a purty penny."

His face filled the window again. I knew that he was aware of my trembling inside and out.

"There's only one way you gonna git outta here," he said. "An' I want you to listen carefully. The best thing you can do is jest turn around and drive back outta here exactly the same way you come in. Don't stop. Don't turn off. Just keep a-goin' till you get all the way back outta here the same way."

He leaned forward glaring into my eyes.

"One thing more. You forget you wuz ever in here."

He paused a few seconds for emphasis.

"You understand?"

"Yes, Sir, I understand," I agreed.

Vastly relieved, I cranked the engine, backed up until I found a place to turn around, then headed out. I glanced in the rear view mirror. The old guy had resumed his military pose in the middle of the road, the shotgun brandished in front of him.

Then, almost in slow motion it seemed, he raised the shotgun in firing position, aimed at me. I floorboarded the accelerator and the old truck lurched forward, flouncing over the rough terrain as I heard the distinct "boom" of a shotgun. Although I slowed down, I didn't stop for two miles until I got to a better road and some civilization.

I never did go back that way, either.

Later, I talked with a man knowledgeable about this community.

"You had a run-in with ol' man Grimes," he said. "He guards the road for them. On down that old road a ways there's several moonshine liquor stills in operation. They operate the year around. They don't like strangers blundering in on them. That old road is the only way in and out. They keep Grimes there guarding it."

"You're lucky. You got out light. Ol' Grimes likes to scare the daylights outta trespassers. Depending on how drunk he is, he'll fire his ol' shotgun at the rear of the vehicle as it's leaving or up in the air and let the pellets fall on top of it. Scares most people silly. An' they don't ever go back either."

I sold my old pickup a year or so later.

The purchaser didn't ask, nor did I volunteer any explanation about the circular pattern of shotgun pellet dents in the tailgate.

UNCLE LUCIAN'S LIGHT

I was almost twelve when my parents let me spend a day with Uncle Lucian, pastor of two country churches, who said he would take me with him visiting. He liked me because he thought I might grow up to become a preacher, which I never did. I liked him because of all the exciting stories I'd heard about his fabulous preaching career.

As we left his rural home that December morning, Aunt Mindy reproached her husband: "You ought to be visiting this needy household. We hardly got nothing left to eat. We need flour and meal, meat and potatoes, coffee, salt, sugar, dry beans, oil for the lamps, wood for the stove, clothes and shoes for the children. I know you ain't got much money, but please come back by the store and bring home what you can. These young'uns are about to starve. Please! Christmas is almost here, you know."

I saw tears on her cheeks. She shoved her arms heaven-ward as if pleading that Heaven might produce better results than would her husband, who appeared unmoved by her plea.

As we walked away, I looked back at the rundown farm-house and saw Ridgely, his teenage son, sitting a-straddle the peak of the roof. I pulled at his arm. "Uncle Lucian, reckon Ridgely might fall and get hurt up there on the roof?"

"Nah, the Lord'll look after him."

The Lord had been looking after Uncle Lucian for a long time. The Lord and the Lord's light. I'd heard the adults talk about it.

Light was the focus and cornerstone of Uncle Lucian's ministry. Always God's divine light. He was launched by light. He died with a halo of light around his head. In between, he, a brick mason, organized congregations, built churches, conducted revivals and tent crusades, dispensed good news and affirmations. He became a living legend throughout the Uwharrie area and beyond. And he did all this despite the enormous handicap of illiteracy. His followers would tell you that while Uncle Lucian never learned to read and write, he could stand in the pulpit and read his scripture passage as fluently as a doctor of theology. He didn't fumble around or hesitate or lose his place. He read it emphatically and with feeling. His expressive way of sermonizing made you pay attention.

"You help God and God helps you," he responded when asked about this uncanny ability. "You do all you can for God. Then do all you can for yourself. God'll help you with the rest. That's God's light a-workin'. That light's always a-workin'."

Always the light. Sometimes he would tell how the light originally shined down on him one dark night and commanded him to preach. Always, he reminded people that God was the light of the world, and the light of that personal world inside each individual. He had memorized all the "light" verses in the Bible and quoted them frequently, especially Matthew 5:14-16.

Amazing, too, was the way all those church building debts got paid. Among ordinary people, money was scarce back in the Great Depression era of the 1930s. But when a new congregation united and determined to build a church—with Uncle Lucian leading the hands-on construction—everything came together. Most of the land, materials, labor and furnishings were donated or bartered. Just enough cash showed up to meet obligations.

Long after Uncle Lucian died, two elderly men revealed a long-kept secret—how, as youngsters, they helped launch his preaching career and initiate his lifelong fascination with divine light.

They were coon hunting one dark night in the edge of some thick woods alongside a country lane. One boy had climbed a tree to look for the coon. Uncle Lucian came walking by the lane on his way home. Abruptly, the boy in the tree turned on a powerful flashlight, its beam shining directly down on Uncle Lucian. Startled, he interpreted it as a divine call to preach, similar to Paul's transforming experience on the Damascus Road. Bewildered and overwhelmed, he dropped to his knees, praying and thanking God.

Stunned by this unexpected action, the boy in the tree made no noise and kept the light shining until Uncle Lucian jumped up shouting and ran home to tell his family about the miraculous light and what it meant to him.

Not wishing to discredit anyone, the boys remained discreetly silent about the incident for decades until long after Uncle Lucian died. Even then, not many people believed their part of the story.

In his late thirties when he started, Uncle Lucian became a preaching phenomenon. He was always off preaching and too busy to farm and help Aunt Mindy and the children with the chores. Despite the success of his ministry, he remained virtually penniless, giving away his money to the less fortunate.

That's why I wondered all day long, with no money in his pocket, how could he meet this crisis at home, Aunt Mindy's ultimatum to bring food and household items from the store back home with him at the end of the day. It worried me, but he didn't appear concerned about it. I mentioned it several times.

"She hasn't seen the light like me," he said. "She gets wrought up. But you and me..." his sparkly old eyes looked hard at me, "...we've seen the light. We know things'll work out."

Since his battered old model-A touring car was broken down and being repaired at a church member mechanic's home, we walked and hitched rides all over one end of the county. We visited church members and non-church people, the sick and shut-in, the dispirited and the prosperous. One household fed us a satisfying country style lunch. At other homes we briefly helped slaughter a hog, cut firewood, nail weatherboarding on a barn, put new shoes on a mule, re-rope the windlass at a dug well. Whatever the household members were doing, we pitched in and helped.

One farmer had just sold a cow and a calf for a tidy sum. He pressed six worn dollar bills into Uncle Lucian's hand. "This is fer you, now," he emphasized.

Oh boy, I exulted to myself. Now he'll have enough money to buy that stuff at the store that Aunt Mindy wants him to bring home.

Late afternoon, we headed toward home. A wizened old man and an energetic youngster. He whistled and sang fragments of hymns, insisting that I accompany him. I never felt happier or more carefree. He let me carry his big tattered Bible part of the way. I felt so proud, carrying the Bible for an important man like Uncle Lucian.

Along the way, he preached to me some and I took it all in, pleased to be the recipient of such sound advice. I'd have plenty to tell my dad and mom when I got home. My dad had always been skeptical of his brother-in-law and harsh with his criticism. Maybe my report of the day's activities would change his mind.

"Don't ever preach a sermon while you're praying," Uncle Lucian said.

He looked at me and talked to me like I was already a practicing preacher.

"Keep praying and preaching separate. They don't mix well. Before a congregation, keep your prayer short and direct. People don't want to stay too long with their heads bowed, their eyes closed, standing or maybe on their knees. So, keep it short. In private praying, you can ramble all you want to, but in public praying, keep it simple.

"In preaching, you can go anywhere you want, ramble all you want, testify all you want, tell stories to illustrate your points—just so you relate all of it to your main theme. In my case that's the light, always the light. I don't ever preach without the light. I don't do anything without the light. Keep your light a-shining every day, every hour, every minute.

"Most everybody has the light. But in some it's dim, almost burned out. Such a shame. They need their wicks trimmed, their globes cleaned, new oil in their lamps. That's our job."

He looked at me.

"We got to unclog them. Remove their burdens and their obstructions so their light can shine free and strong all the time. Yeah...we gotta help 'em do that."

Our last stop was to see the widow McCall, whose no-good husband had run off leaving her with a baby and a seven-year-old son to raise. She and the baby were sick in bed, moaning, almost convulsing. "I've got to get some medicine from town and a few things," she gasped. "My little Johnny could run in and get it for me...if we just had some money..."

Six worn dollar bills were pressed into the woman's hand. My heart sank. He prayed fervently for God's healing power to begin work and for the restoration of health and light to this household.

Quick as we got out of earshot, I voiced my dismay. "But, Uncle Lucian, now how you gonna buy that stuff Aunt Mindy told you to bring home?"

He looked at me reproachfully. "You'll understand better when you see the light more clearly," he said. "Acts like that," he jerked his hand over his shoulder, "that generates more fuel for the light."

We walked right on past the country store without stopping.

When we got in sight, Aunt Mindy stood on the porch watching for us. She could tell we had no bags or parcels, just that Bible under Uncle Lucian's arm. It looked like her shoulders drooped as she vanished inside.

"She'll be disappointed and mad at us," I predicted. I wished I could hide in the bushes and wait a while so I wouldn't have to hear Aunt Mindy berating Uncle Lucian for failing to bring home the bacon. But I didn't. I guess I could take it if he could. I almost tiptoed across the porch as we went inside.

"Look, look!" the children yelled. Some of them clapped their hands. The little ones jumped up and down.

"Yes, look," Aunt Mindy said, smiling and waving her hands around the room. "Both your congregations pounded you today. They been bringing stuff the whole blessed day. They said it was long overdue."

That room looked like a grocery and dry goods store. My heart beat fast. My eyes bulged. Never had I seen anything like this.

Sacks of flour, meal, potatoes, peanuts, cabbage, corn, fruit; bags of sugar, salt, coffee, lard, soap, scores of jars of canned food, big slabs of cured meat, bolts of cloth, needles and thread, clothing and shoes for everyone, a new lamp and lantern, plus cans of oil. Outside under the shelter, the men had stacked two two-horse wagon loads of firewood and split stove wood.

Uncle Lucian looked a bit stunned and humbled by it all. He slipped the big Bible into my hands temporarily. As I watched a beaming Aunt Mindy hugging her husband with all their children gathered around, a yellowish light shimmered into a halo shape above them. Faint angel singing came from somewhere. If any heavenly hosts lurked about, they had to be praising the Lord for all this happiness. I didn't mind the tears on my face because I was so amazed and thrilled for them.

This was so much more than Aunt Mindy had asked for, even dreamed about. It assured them of a comfortable Christmas. The magnitude of such a pounding would launch Uncle

Lucian into a newer, higher orbit of preaching and proclaiming–powered by that divine light.

A strange sensation began creeping up my arms and into my body. It started with a tingle, then grew into liquid fire, like a benevolent blaze purging me from my scalp to my toes. I knew where it came from, too, and my heart hammered at this realization. It came from that big Bible I held in my arms. Against my chest, that Bible pulsated with warmth and empowering energy, just for me. And I knew what was happening, too. A spiritual ball of fire. Illumination. Revelation. A perpetual inner glow.

I was experiencing that light Uncle Lucian always talked about.

THE SMOOTH STONE MAN

I couldn't believe my eyes when this obscure road deadended at a modest home amid a thin grove of trees near a creek. Piles of rocks everywhere. At first, I assumed these piles were randomly located. But then I began to see some order in their arrangement. As I stood there gawking, a strange human figure shuffled into sight from behind one pile. He appeared startled at my presence. Obviously, he didn't get many visitors in this isolated corner of the Uwharries.

That's how I met the Smooth Stone Man.

From his scuffed brogans up, soiled trousers and shirt which tried to swallow his angular frame. Ragged holes exposed his knees and elbows. A brush pile moustache hid most of his face. Whiskers, brushy eyebrows and long hair streaked with gray carpeted the remainder. His hands looked like big calloused grain scoops.

I told him I wanted to look around at his stones. He nodded and shuffled along with me.

Most of us have seen thin smooth-sided stones of varying size, worn that way by years of tumbling and scouring amid finer gravel in a stream bed. Flowing stream water causes this movement and this natural sculpture. But probably not many of us have seen tons and tons of such stones displayed in myriad imaginative uses around a household.

The longer we walked around his premises, the more amazed I became at what he had done with these stones.

He had used them as thick borders along walkways, paths and trails, around flower beds and tree trunks. He had paved his driveway with stones and underpinned his house with them. His yard featured stone pyramids and towers, a shallow stone fish pond, stone foundations and benches and tables, stone outlines of pirate ships, dragons and various structures. Even the exterior of his house, chimney and outbuildings had been veneered with smooth stones. Smooth stone retaining walls outlined his vegetable garden and part of his yard. Smooth stone steps led to the doors of his dwelling. Near the creek bank, a smooth stone chair invited you to sit and fish or meditate.

Back off the creek bank, several piles and stacks of smooth stones awaited utilization.

"Where did you collect all these smooth stones?" I asked.

"Up and down the creek there," he motioned.

His voice sounded clacky, like the crack-kk sound made when you crack a walnut.

"But how did you get 'em here?" I asked. "You didn't tote 'em by hand, did you?"

I imagined a grin under the hairy maze of his face.

"Nope. I use my wheelbarr' and my ol' pickup."

I could see the rusty tailgate of an ancient pickup truck sticking out of the shed behind his house. Interested in old vehicles, I asked to see his truck. He backed it out into the yard.

Smooth stones decorated the entire vehicle.

A line of them went down the middle of the hood. Appropriately sized smooth stones had replaced the headlights and review mirrors. A stone had been fitted into the center of each wheel. Smaller stones outlined the wheel wells and door bottoms. Stones protruded along the top edge of the bed. Several unattached stones lay across the dashboard, more on the floor.

"How do you get the stones to stick fast?" I asked.

"Big secret", he chuckled. "I pulverize some of these stones into a power and mix it with the mortar. Makes it lots stronger."

He used his fist to pound against one stone on the edge of the pickup bed.

"Here, you try it." He handed me an oak limb big as a mattock handle. "Go on, hit...hard."

I struck a medium blow on the rock, then two more, each one harder. "Harder," he urged.

I wound up like a baseball batter hitting a grand slammer and gave the stone a terrific blow, all the muscle might I had in it. The whole truck shook.

The top half of the stone cracked and broke off, leaving the bottom half still permanently gripped by its thin layer of ad-hesive mortar.

"How do you loosen that mortar, so you can take off the broken stone and replace it?" I asked.

"'Nother big secret," he said. But he didn't elaborate.

I watched a rawboned hound dog stretch himself out the door of a smooth stone doghouse. A flock of chickens used a smooth stone enclosure for roosting and laying eggs. A home-made wagon with a sideplanked bed overflowed with smooth stones.

We walked to an unused stack of stones and I examined a few. They ranged in size from a quarter to a silver dollar, on to the top of a drinking glass to a saucer and dinner plate. Many were about the size of your palm and oval shaped. None were more than an inch or two thick. All had smooth edges and sides. No major flaws or imperfections were apparent.

"What do you do with the ones that have flaws on them?" I asked.

"Throw 'em back in the creek and let 'em age some more," he responded.

He had devised his own tumbler to help nature speed up the smoothing process. I marveled at the cleverness of its engineering design.

Across the creek he had built a dam of smooth stones and other rocks. About midway, the creek flow was channeled through a narrow gap, the water falling a few feet below. Down there he had excavated a wide hole and filled it with fine gravel from the creek bed. Flawed stones were thrown into this loose gravel bed by the hundreds. The permanent spillover water flow kept the stones and the gravel in constant agitated motion, which soon scrubbed away the imperfections. Regularly, he removed the finished stones and added rougher ones.

I asked about the shuffle in his walking.

He pulled up his pants leg exposing a knot on the side of his leg caused by the improper healing of an unset broken leg bone.

"Stack of stones fell off the creek bank on top of me. Broke my leg. Trapped me there in the creek for hours before I wiggled loose. Almost drowned."

I stood with my arm extended and motioned around in a circle. "You did all this, all by yourself?"

"All by myself," he nodded.

I learned later that his wife and children left him and moved away because of his preoccupation with the smooth stones. "That's all he would do, just play around with them durn rocks in the creek," a former neighbor told me. "Daylight to dark that's all he would do."

"How long have you been fooling around with the smooth stones here like this?" I asked the Smooth Stone Man.

"Twenty years, I reckon," he said. "Started when I was about forty or forty-five." He looked around, his eyes caressing all the stones in sight. "Wonder if I got another twenty to go...."

When I left, he insisted that I take a handful of smooth stones. For years, I kept them prominently displayed at home until the grandchildren appropriated them for some obscure use.

I know this will never happen, but even today, if I thought I could ever find the Smooth Stone Man location again, I would hire a tractor-trailer and bring out an eighteen-wheeler-load of smooth stones and make a fortune selling them at flea markets for artists to paint pictures on.

REAL SPECIAL VIGG-A

I first met Smithie after we left town and moved into an old farmhouse in the edge of the Uwharries. He drove into our backyard one afternoon and wormed his way out of a rattletrap car which backfired and made him jump about the time he cleared it. Tall and thin, he had a long face, missing teeth and happy eyes. John Barleycorn wafted out strong on his breath. His first steps were a bit unsteady. Then, he stabilized and leaned against our picnic table, his face glistening in tranquil reminiscence.

"I'm Smithie," he said in a sort've meowy voice. "I used to come here and buy stuff from Mista Byrd."

He looked up like he was addressing a whole skyful of listeners.

"Mista Byrd used to have lots of stuff to sell out heah," he meowed in a mellow voice so drawly it made Freddie, my first grade son, and me exchange glances and grin behind his back.

"'Taters and 'maters," he enumerated, staring toward the barn. "Peas and corn. Uummm, um, some of the best sweet corn you evah sunk a tooth in. Sweet 'taters! Lawdy, he had sweet 'taters by the wagonload, so smacking good we et 'em snoot raw. An' watermelons and mus'melons! Never been no better 'uns. Peanuts! Big ol' fat red goobers with lots of squish in 'em. Boy, you could et a handful of 'em goobers and feel jist like a—a King!"

He stood there looking off into the sky, lost in his gastronomical reverie.

47

I signaled silence to Freddie. He understood. Let Smithie talk.

"Apples. He had apples just a-tumbling everwhere. Good apples. Sound 'uns. When you bought his apples, he let you pick 'em out. He didn't mind if you culled out the knotty 'uns and put better 'uns in their place. He used the knotty 'uns in cider, anyway. When you got weary of apples, he'd sell you cider. Made lots of cider, that ol' man did. Good cider. Sweet or a little hard and aged. Take your pick. Charged a few cents extra for the jug, 'less you promised faithful to bring it back. All of us wondered what he did with the cider that got too hard to sell. Made vinegar out of it, I reckon."

He turned and looked hard at me, sensing that I may have caught a wrong implication in his words.

"He didn't drink any hard stuff. Mista Byrd was no drunkard. No, sir-ee. Good ol' man. Oh, he'd drink some cider. Maybe a little homemade wine now and then. I'spect he'd taste a little high-grade moonshine, too."

Here, he stopped and contemplated a moment, like maybe he, himself, would like to go back to those high-grade moonshine days.

"Mista Byrd was honest and reasonable. Didn't try to rob nobody. What he charged was fair. But he wanted his money. If you bought somethin', boy he expected his money right then. I've heard him tell his customers, especially us customers from over my way, an' 'specially during them yummy watermelon and mus'melon times. He'd say, 'Boys, now I'm a-selling you these melons cheap enough. You can afford to buy them. I don't want nobody a-stealin' from me. If I catch anybody a-foolin' 'round in that watermelon patch, I'm a-gonna let 'em have both barrels of that twelve-gauge shotgun standing yonder right inside my back door. You tell everybody that now and be sure they understand it. What I sell you, I sell you fair. But I ain't gonna have no stealin'. I'll doublebarrel you in a minute!' I never knowed nobody stealin' from 'im either."

He nodded his white-matted head at some contemplated logic known only to him. "I miss that ol'man," he said.

His tall frame jerked in a start, then he turned and appeared to loosen up allover, and bubble. He clapped his hands softly. His old eyes were not just happy and bright now, they were singing eyes.

I knew immediately what had captured his fancy.

Coming into sight between the barn and the corncrib was a flock of nondescript hens domineered by a robust rooster we called Clarence because of his clarion-like crowing. Ol' Clarence was mean, sneaky, and arrogant. He'd as soon flog you and sink his spurs into you as not. He constantly annoyed the hens. I've heard a lot of roosters crow, but ol' Clarence had the most devastating ear-shrilling crow I can remember. I'll bet you could hear it a mile. Even the hens would sometimes run from his crowing. I've seen visitors jab fingers in their ears when he crowed near them.

Sensing a stranger present, ol' Clarence reared back, took a deep breath and let loose a crow that reverberated the rafters and shook dust out of the inside top of the nearby barn.

Smithie's face glistened in delight. Admiration for this randy rooster shined in his eyes. He dropped to his knees and tried to entice the rooster closer.

"You got what I been looking for," Smithie breathed excitedly. "Hens that run wid a rooster. An' what a rooster! Man, he is one more he-boar rooster."

He watched, fascinated, while ol' Clarence proved his virility by mounting a hen.

"Them hens do lay eggs, don't they?"

I nodded "Yeah, in fact we have a small surplus of eggs now."

"This is my lucky day," Smithie breathed. "I just gotta have some of them eggs. I'll buy a dozen right now. For a long time, I ben lookin' for some good ol' country eggs from hens that run wid a rooster. An' I has found 'em. Man, what a rooster."

Without taking his eyes off the rooster, he continued talking,

"For a long time, I ben rundown and doing porely. Nothing has hepped me. Nothing will till I get hold of some of these eggs. I been lookin' for some eggs like this for months. They'll help me. Eggs from hens that dat run wid a rooster like this ol' boy are rich, man. Rich and powerful. I swallow them raw and I eats' em cooked, too. Makes me feel good all over. Makes me long-winded and gives me vigg-a."

He emphasized the last word.

He glanced at Freddie and pulled me to one side out of respect for Freddie's tender age.

"Eggs like this gives you real special vigg-a, you know," he said, winking at me dramatically.

He paid us for a dozen eggs and left almost dancing a jig as he programmed his lanky frame back into his small car a section at a time.

A week later he was back for more eggs. After that, he came back regularly for more eggs until our flock finally dwindled and evaporated. Each time he had glowing testimony at how much improved his personal health was, altogether due to eating these eggs laid by hens that run with a rooster, especially a he-boar rooster like ol' Clarence.

Always, he walked around the premises till he found the flock and he stood there admiring ol' Clarence while he crowed and mounted hens.

Every visit he would pull me aside so Freddie and his mother couldn't hear and give me the lowdown.

"It's 'mazing, man, it's just 'mazing. Them eggs is giving me real special vigg-a like nothing else ever has. An' I do mean *real special vigg-a!*"

He winked at me grandly and chortled fiendishly.

Smithie expressed concern about the dwindling flock and the reduced supply of eggs and its effect on his future personal vigg-a. He wanted to bring in more hens. He said let's round up another rooster or two, comparable to ol' Clarence, and triple the size of the original flock. He could bring more customers. Up to now, he had not disclosed the secret of his vastly improved libido, but with increased production and ready availability of these eggs, he could share with his male friends and generate a steady stream of eager customers. They'd pay extra for these special eggs, too.

Briefly, I considered it. But instinct tugged at me negatively. Too much hassle. I told Smithie I was tired of chicken raising; that he'd have to get his own flock.

When the flock dwindled to one mousy hen, glassy-eyed and debilitated from the rooster's constant attention, I gave them both to Smithie. The prospects of having ol' Clarence for a meal left him awestricken. I could almost see the wheels turning in his head as he tried to compute how much more real special vigg-a eating ol' Clarence would give him.

Since Freddie wasn't old enough to understand the significance of the vigg-a part, he and I kidded his mother about the type of eggs we wanted to keep us long-winded and healthy.

Privately, I tell her that the only type of eggs I want in our household henceforth are eggs from hens that run with a rooster, so I can maintain my own real special vigg-a.

And depending on the mood she's in, I wink at her grandly and chortle like Smithie did at me.

THE TREE PAINTER

From a quarter-mile away all I could see was a human figure busy among some large trees near his home in a streak of level bottomland alongside a creek. Instinct told me to move in for a closer look. I left the secondary dirt road and descended the rougher approach road which deadended at his home. He saw me approaching, then pretended to ignore me.

What he was doing was painting pictures on tree trunks, big, living, upright tree trunks.

I wouldn't have believed it, either, had I not witnessed it right there in the real world of the Uwharrie backwoods.

This middle-aged guy wearing sawed-off blue jean shorts, and no shirt sat on a rickety stool. He leaned forward to work intently, then reared back to evaluate in constant repetitive motion. Sweat-streaked hair tangled down to merge with brows and beard to create a sheep-shearing gray maze of fluffiness around his face and head. I wondered if sparks from his piercing eyes might ignite that tinderbox of gray.

When the work progressed upward, he had to stand to reach it, then climb atop the stool which gave him several more feet of reaching space. His stretching and leaning made the stool creak and protest under his dirty bare feet. Flab bulged over the straining waistband of his shorts. A paint rag flapped from a rear pocket.

While he whistled and hummed at his work, I looked and looked.

With the musical gurgling of the creek in the background, I walked among the dozen or so big-trunked trees in the half-acre plot where he worked. All these trees had smooth bark and no limbs and few imperfections for the first ten or twelve feet. About half already had pictures painted on them. These pictures spiraled ever upward in continuity as if they were painted on a tower or lighthouse. Once or twice I experienced brief dizziness as I sidestepped around a tree with my head crannied upward. Some of the uncompleted pictures vanished into the foliage, which made you want to linger and figure it out. Or find a ladder and climb up there.

The subject matter fascinated me, as did the obvious artistic skill of the painter.

Wild animals in various poses, some menacing, circled the tree trunks. A monkey swung from a vine. An elephant spread its bulk around the tree. A giraffe's neck wrapped twice around the tree, it's head vanishing into the foliage. A rooster reared back to crow. Farm and domestic animals, broken down farm implements, dilapidated farm structures, hills, valleys, streams, cliffs, waterfalls, cabins, fences, wild flowers—all were represented in refreshing detail on the tree trunks. Most of one trunk portrayed huge, bulky wrestlers and boxers. Follow-the-leader buzzards circled up another trunk. One tree featured a descending figure, a fiery-eyed monster belching fire and froth from a needle-toothed mouth opened to swallow you.

All this in color, too.

I was past the amazement stage; I was stunned by the magnitude of it all.

The tree painter caught my eye and beckoned me hither. He nodded upward and I looked. Up there, he had painted me, crannied neck and all, onto the tree trunk, including part of my old pickup. A good likeness, indeed.

Break time came and I learned more about this incredible character.

Five years ago, he started painting on tree trunks with mud and soft rocks, using his fingers to manipulate the mud. He liked it so much he experimented with berries, fruits, flowers and herbs, using store-bought brushes. Then everything became homemade. He developed a formula for making and mixing his own paint, perfecting several colors. He made his own palette and brushes. The subjects he painted on tree trunks came spontaneously right out of his mind.

"I can see it," he said, tapping his head with the brush handle. "When I can see it up here, then I can put it on the trees. In color, too."

His voice sounded slightly shrill, as if he were a bit hyper. Did he ever paint on canvas or paper?

"No, just the trees. Trees are challenging."

How long did the paintings stay in place on the tree trunks?

"Till it rains," was his short answer.

All his homemade paint was designed to wash off when doused with water. A heavy downpour of rain would loosen and wash off all the paint on the tree trunks. Soon as the surface dried, usually by the next day, it was ready for fresh paint and pictures.

"Do you ever run out of trees before it rains?" I asked.
"Yep," he shrilled.

"Well, then how do you keep painting?"

He looked at me with scorn in his eyes and voice.

"Look over there," he motioned.

Over there lay a pile of buckets—half-bushel buckets, five-gallon buckets, gallon buckets, all rusty and tarnished from use. Two fifty-five-gallon metal drums and a wooden barrel formed a backdrop.

"Plenty of water in the creek," he nodded.

So, when the rains didn't come often enough to suit him, and his painting passion kept raging, he toted water from the creek to splash on the tree paintings to dissolve them.

Mentally, he kept track of the sequence of his tree trunk paintings. He started his bucket splashing on the oldest and continued day by day until the rains came.

I counted about a dozen trees.

"How long does it take you to paint 'em all up?" I asked.

"Two-three weeks," he said. "One a day is about my average."

He said fog, mist and moisture-filled air sometimes caused his freshest paintings to run and streak, ruining everything below.

"Wish it would run *up*," he said, whimsey softening his voice. "But it won't. Gravity, you know."

Once, he painted all morning and reached the halfway point at noon. After the noon break, he started to finish the painting but a rainstorm interfered and washed away his morning work. This continued every day for a week.

"Frustrating," he said. "Gets you riled."

Did he ever run out of mental pictures to transfer to the tree trunks?

"Na, the only thing I run out of is trees," he said. "I need more trees. And daylight."

He reflected a moment.

"I try it at night sometimes. Hang up a lighted oil lantern to see by. But it never works. Just can't paint right at night. Gotta have good daytime light."   .

He chuckled.

"A few folks passing on the road up here have seen my light at night and they think it might be ghosts a-coming to look at my painting."

"Why don't you put a gate across your road up here and charge admission to people to come down here and look at you painting pictures on trees? This is amazing."

"Na. I ain't got no time for a gate or charging people. They can come if they want to. You did. All I wanna do is paint."

To prove it, he ignored me and went back to his work. Fascination held me there a little longer.

Homemade paint, brushes, and palette. A head full of mental pictures. A pile of buckets. A gurgling creek. A rickety, squeaky stool. Washed-off gunk and debris around the bottom of each tree. A line around the tree trunk where the top edge of the stool scarred the bark when the whistling, humming painter stood atop it. Uncompleted pictures mysteriously vanishing into the foliage.

Somehow, I wondered if I was dreaming, though I knew for certain I stood there witnessing all of this taking place. A strange yellowish glimmer, faint and pulsating, seemed to merge with grayish ghostliness around the tree painter's face and head.

When I left, he handed me a piece of smooth bark about the size of a shoebox lid. On it he had painted a miniature profile of me and the front of my old pickup. I tried to pay him for it. He just waved goodbye with the paint brush in his hand.

I kept the bark portrait on a shelf over my desk until it disintegrated into a pile of rubble and dust and my wife made me move it.

I understand some pictures still appear on smooth barked trees in the Uwharries. Maybe ghosts are doing it.

Or maybe the passionate ghost of the old tree painter has learned how to paint trees at night.

THE MAN WHO MADE SUNSHINE

Unfortunately, I never got to meet the man who made sunshine. He was long gone before I began my research. But I did meet many cherished memories of him. These memories painted such vivid imagery in my mind that they generated an overswell of camaraderie. I felt that he wanted me to get to know him intimately, which I did. You can get to know him too....

Gabriel's face glowed with unusual luminosity as he entered the modest home of the widow McCall on the outskirts of the Uwharrie community. Bushy-browed eyes twinkled. His wide smile erased creases and age lines on his weathered countenance. His nose pushed out from his face like a boulder on the side of Dark Mountain. Grayish hair swirled around his head. One big hand guarded the top of a glass container partly concealed under his arm. A yellowish glow from this container matched the radiance in his face.

Gabriel was on a mission.

Nearing 80, the widow McCall looked as if she saw the Death Messenger beckoning her into a dark chamber. Unruly white hair fell in knotty tangles around her pallid face, punctuated by a pair of feverish eyes. As she sat on the edge of the bed, her open-topped gown revealed skeletonized bones around her shoulders and neck. A scrawny hand tried to push the gown back in place as she greeted her visitor.

"That you, Gabe?" Her voice sounded like a dying calf. "They told me you might come. But it's too late. Sho', it's too late. Nothing can help me now. I done seen death's angel a-beckoning me on."

"Never too late, Aunt Swiney," Gabe rejoined. "Never too late. We gonna help you get better. Right quick, too. That's why we here. You'll see."

"Nobody bin here for a week. No vittles for two days. My chill'un may come in another week er so. 'Course, it's too late then. Oh-h-h-h me! This ol' grip is sho' a-grippin' me..."

Her voice rambled into incoherence.

Gabe moved closer as he removed the top from the quart-sized glass jar under his arm. He lifted it beside his face. Radiance rushed out toward the sick woman. A warm glow surrounded her for a few seconds, and then diminished. Gabe re-capped the container and supported it under his arm, the sleeve of his jacket partly hiding it. Quietly he left the house.

A few hours later, someone saw the widow McCall dressed and groomed, a basket dangling from her arm, enroute to the local general store for shopping. They say she hummed a tune, walked briskly and waved at passersby.

A miracle?

Yes, older Uwharrians say, a miracle brought about by the sunshine from Gabriel's jar.

Until he died well over a hundred years ago, Gabriel and his jar of sunshine must have helped hundreds of country people over half a century or more. Whatever the ailment or condition, he could help. Seldom did he miss an opportunity to help his fellowman. Gabe and his jar. Always the jar. One couldn't work without the other. Hardly anyone remains today who has ever heard of the story of the man who made sunshine.

"That's the way I've heard it told," an old man reminisces. "He packed sunshine into that jar, then loosed it to help ailing people, 'cause my grandpappy was among 'em."

Packing sunshine into a jar? Keeping it? Controlling it? Using it medically, therapeutically? Could that be done, even today?

Gabriel never flaunted his skills and abilities. He just let them flow, which almost always produced the results desired. Nothing ostentatious. Naturalness permeated everything he did. And all he did was open for everyone to examine, analyze, judge, and marvel at. Instinct guided him, while nature motivated.

Whenever you saw Gabriel, you saw the jar, too. Often, when no patient needed help, the top of the jar remained open, apparently left open on purpose. Did it collect and absorb sunshine this way? People affirmed that always you could see a faint, yellowish glimmer inside the jar, even on rainy days, even at night, even inside a dark house.

So, how did sunshine accumulate in Gabe's jar on sunless days?

Nobody ever figured this out. He shared this secret with no one. But after a week or more with no sun, the jar continued functioning just as well as on bright days.

While occasionally someone summoned him, most of the time Gabe seemed to know when and where he and his jar were needed. Not always did he respond immediately. He relied on instinct and some signal from a higher place to tell him when to go. And sometimes he wouldn't go at all, because the signs weren't right.

When Bismark Dunlap's son, Maydak, fell out of the hayloft, hit the corn planter and injured himself internally, he could have lain there for hours before anyone found him. But Gabe knew. He arrived about the time family members got home and discovered the accident. Gabe spoke a few words, opened the jar, lifted it beside his face and pointed it toward the unconscious youngster. Almost immediately Maydak responded. He opened his eyes, sat up, rubbed his sore midriff and wanted to know what happened.

While physical ailments responded to Gabe and his jar, psychological conditions responded even better.

Maebell Dicey couldn't cope with emotional trauma after her lover deserted her. Her family asked Gabe to intervene. He focused his jar's sunshine on her and spoke reassuring words. Maebell became such a livewire in her community that she attracted numerous suitors.

Disappointment, bereavement, disorientation, over-indulgence, laziness, retardation, dementia, resentments, and other mental and emotional conditions cleared up after exposure to Gabe and the contents of his jar.

People shook their heads in amazement, gratitude in their faces. The country doctor seldom came around anymore. He said they didn't need him with Gabe on the scene. The itinerant country preacher said Gabe had a divine gift and that the Lord guided him in its use. Convinced of Gabe's authenticity, the preacher encouraged ailing people to patronize him. Word spread and suffering people from distant places came to the Uwharries seeking help from this man who used sunshine to heal. Some mornings found a cluster of people waiting at his modest home. Gloomy days or bright, he helped them all.

All commented on the yellowish glimmer coming from the open jar pointed toward them for a few seconds from near his radiant face.

Observant people knew Gabe kept his jar open during whatever positive activity he encountered. So, the jar was exposed to a lot—smiles, laughter, singing, music, the exuberance of children, the charisma of adults, the steadfastness of the determined, the glow of the spiritually attuned, the intelligence of the elite, the love and serenity of the truly inspired.

"Gabe was letting the sunshine in—that's what he called it, my grandpappy said," the old man continued. "He kept that jar charged and ready."

The jar must have had an astounding storage capacity. It never became exhausted. Always it maintained its potency for healing and restoration under the guidance of its master. Energized by the good, it counteracted the bad.

If Gabe and the jar refused to get involved in a case, this was a good indication the case was terminal, that it had been divinely programmed and that remedial effort was useless. Gabe always seemed to know. Everyone trusted his judgment.

The preacher brought him one difficult case, a disbeliever. This man's agnosticism had ostracized him in the community, although he cared not a whit what his peers thought about his philosophy and his lifestyle. But the preacher considered the man an infidel, feared he might influence others in this direction, so he wanted Gabe to intervene. It took Gabe several attempts to make any headway. Folks said the sunshine inside

Gabe's jar even dimmed a bit under the strain. Eventually, sunshine prevailed. On the day the transition occurred, the man experienced a painful physical malady and sought Gabe and his jar for relief. Not only did his pain go away, but he shrugged off his agnosticism along with it, rejoicing and praising Gabe and his jar for spreading spiritual sunshine.

As Gabe aged, his use of the sunshine jar subsided. Community leaders urged him to continue, promising help in recruiting and training a younger person to assist him. But no suitable replacement ever surfaced. Gabe grew old, infirm and died without ever revealing the details about his ministry. There is some belief that the sunshine jar kept him active and contributed to his longevity well beyond the average mortality rate for that era.

An old country preacher is credited with a final observation and tribute to Gabe in his eulogy.

"Gabe could have done it just as well without the jar. Yes, he could. The jar was just a ploy. A psychological ploy. And it worked. It caught and held their attention and helped them accept and believe. Believing–that's the key. But the real sunshine, the real power, came from Gabe's face, his radiant beaming face, reflecting a divinely powerful spirituality–from his eyes, his soothing voice, his personality, his total Godly being. This is what caused that jar to appear to glow and shine on the patient for a few seconds. It came from Gabe. It was his own personal sunshine. A man so deeply energized by God and goodness that he created sunshine...and gave it away.

"And you know what? Most everybody can do the same thing. If you try. If you want to enough. If you work at it. Sure, you can.

"And you know what else?

"You don't even need a glass jar like ol' Gabe used. You don't need any sort of receptacle. You don't need nothing in your hands. You've already got the container you need, the only one you'll ever need. That container is you. Your body, your heart, mind, soul, and your entire life experience. Your total emotional and spiritual essence and capacity. You can soak up sunshine all the time wherever you are. Likewise you can release and spread sunshine all the time wherever you are. Don't try to store it or preserve it for some distant future use. Release it. NOW! Spontaneously. Let it flow through you. You get it freely, so release it freely."

The preacher continued, "Learn to recognize and appreciate all the sunshine pouring into your life, your container, from every source, much of it from people: handshakes, smiles, laughter, hugs, merriment, harmony, compliments, sharing and caring, the dignity and respect you get from gentle and polite people, the exuberance and adoration from children, angelic music and singing that thrills your soul, a sermon or talk that touches your innermost being, a perfect sunrise or sunset, nature's spectacular scenery, that glorious individual who is so wholesome, pure and radiant that he or she must represent the pinnacle of God's creation.

"This is the sunshine that you collect in your container. This is the sunshine that you release to other people. Most of us are around other people most of the time, family members, loved ones, neighbors, friends, fellow workers, even strangers. Practice releasing your sunshine to these people spontaneously and in creative ways. And do it anonymously, unobtrusively, without the recipient or anyone else knowing what you're doing. Nobody else needs to know. This is your own personal ministry.

"And if you happen not to be around people, you're alone and you still want to spread sunshine, here's another way. All of us know someone in need, someone we want to help, someone we highlight in our prayers and meditations. As we pray and meditate, let's surround this person with a big, bright warm halo of sunshine and then beam our prayer into this sunshine to activate it and bring relief and improvement to this individual.

"As we practice this method of releasing our sunshine, we can become instruments of healing, just like ol' Gabe—each one of us can become a person who makes sunshine and gives it away."

THE SHOO FLY MAN

Half a day of spring plowing, the old way where you walk behind the turning plow stock pulled by mules or horses, had exhausted this farm family when I stopped at their isolated home at lunchtime on this humid day. They had just left the fields, fed and watered the animals at the barn and were on their way to the dwelling house when I got out of my pickup to greet them. I knew they were too tired, dirty, and hungry to bother with me right at this time. But I had to make my pitch.

"Name's Morgan," I said. "I'm traveling through this part of the country collecting stories about the old days. I'd like to talk with you a while when you have time. Meanwhile, is there anything I can do to help?"

The older man, apparently the father, took off his straw hat, flapped dust off his overalls and wiped sweat off his face with a sleeved forearm. Around him stood four children, two boys and two girls. All wore dirty overalls, straw hats and brogan shoes. All had impatient expressions on their faces.

"We ain't got no time for such as that," he snapped, irritation rasping his voice. "We been in that field hard at work since daylight. Just stopped to eat dinner and rest a bit and let the mules eat."

He took another hard look at me. "You look pale and thin and a little peaked—have you had your dinner yet?"

"No sir, I haven't eaten anything since early this morning," I said.

"Then you can eat with us. Come on, let's wash up and go eat. Ma's done got it ready. Bertie, you run tell Ma to set another plate. We got company."

Washing up occurred on a shelf across one end of the back porch of the ramshackle dwelling. A chipped wash basin sat beside a wooden bucket filled with well water, the handle of a gourd dipper jostling from it. A worn cake of homemade soap occupied a greasy spot on the shelf. A dirty towel dangled dejectedly from a nail on the wall. Each washer-upper dashed the previous washer-upper's dirty water out in the yard before dipping clean water in the basin for himself. All of us went through this process.

Inside, we went through the kitchen, still hot from the dying fire in the old wood burning cook stove, thence into the dining room dominated by a rectangular table laden with good old country food. I sat on one side between two children, the other two across the table. Mother and father sat on either end. We all began to fill our plates and eat heartily.

Immediately, I sensed something amiss. Then I knew.

A rustling noise—dozens of dangles from a low-hanging bar—started at one end of the table and fluttered over the food to the other end of the table. Then it rose up out of the way. Bent over with a forkful of food halfway to my mouth, I had to jerk back to keep the dangles from slapping me in the face. The children giggled at me.

But it worked!

Now I realized what it was.

It was a moveable contraption to shoo the houseflies off the food. And, boy was it needed.

The flies covered everything. And then I knew why. There were no screens over the doors and windows in the old house. All the doors and windows stood wide open for ventilation, to capture whatever vagrant breeze that stirred through the countryside on this stifling hot day.

Of course, the open doors and windows let in more than a random breeze. More than houseflies, too. While there at the table I saw a horsefly lazily buzzing around, grasshoppers, wasps, mosquitoes, wheat bugs, dragon flies, dirt-daubers, bumble bees, lady bugs, a carpenter beetle, gnats, even a small bird flew in one open window and back out through the open door.

All this appeared to be routine to the family members. They paid no attention to the pests. All of them ate food like crazy, pausing only when the dangles fluttered by. I was told that this occurred at every meal, hot weather or cold.

Coming into the room, I vaguely remembered a contraption on the ceiling directly over the dining table, but paid little attention to it then. Now I scrutinized it.

This man and his sons used old boards, pieces of metal, channels, small wheels, pulleys, and ropes to construct a framework on the ceiling. Two vertical bars came down from it, one on either side, to connect a horizontal bar at the bottom. Guided by the channels above, this smaller frame was designed to roll the entire length of the bigger frame above, covering all the table area below. Dangles from the low horizontal bar were made from strips of paper, fabric, twine, ribbons, worn out clothing, anything that would move freely and rustle. So, with the jerk of a cord or the pedal of a foot, the dangles could be made to flutter across the food and scare the flies away, then rise up out of the way until they were needed to go back across the food to the other end of the table.

Engrossed and amazed at this clever contraption, I probably ate some flies along with my food as I sat there and marveled at the ingenuity required to build this unique shoo fly gizmo. The man and woman, the children too, were nonchalant about it, indicating long experience with its effectiveness.

The flies had adapted well, too.

All the flies waited till the last tiniest fraction of a second to leave before the dangles arrived. Once the dangles passed, they re-swarmed over the food faster than a team of football bullies tackling the ball carrier.

Diners, who had to bend their head and shoulders back briefly for the dangles to pass, had time only for a forkful or two of food before the next invasion. If the dangles were too slow coming back, the negligent operator would be verbally reprimanded to "send it!" Practiced synchronization covered everything.

We finished eating and stood. I looked long at this inimitable shoo fly creation while the woman removed all the dirty dishes and spread a big tablecloth over all the uneaten leftover food on the table, thus denying the flies access. The dangles, pulled up high and out of the way, were silent until the next meal.

When I got home that evening, I told my wife about the shoo-fly dangles. She would hardly believe it. Kidding her later, I threatened to build a shoo-fly contraption on the ceiling over the dining table at our house as a conversation piece and imply to visitors it was an ancient holdover from our primitive past.

But I never did. She never would agree to it. Anyway, she reminded me, we have screens over all our doors and windows.

Thank goodness!

OLD TIME BILL COLLECTOR

A robust, middle-aged man nicknamed "Scrappy" did all types of handyman work in our small town back in the 1930s and 1940s. He became widely known through our section of the Uwharries for his odd job versatility. He would build kitchen cabinets, clean out your dug well, level your floor, replace windows and doors, patch your leaky roof, relocate your outhouse.

He did quality work and did it promptly. But some people were slow about paying him. A few tried to stall off payment forever. And this frustrated Scrappy.

One spring, an upper-class homeowner decided he wanted a new fireplace and chimney added to the side of his home. He engaged Scrappy to do the work. They agreed on a price.

Always working alone, Scrappy labored for days on the job. He built the fireplace, hearth and chimney, plus all the related work, to the homeowner's complete satisfaction. But payment was delayed.

Scrappy knew this homeowner had a reputation of weaseling out of his debts, so he was determined to collect. Months passed without payment. Inquiries and reminders were evaded. Scrappy just bided his time, knowing he would get his money when the time was right.

Along about October, cold weather prompted the homeowner to try out his new fireplace. He laid kindling, logs and lit it with splinters of rich pine, expecting a roaring fire to throw warmth out into the room.

Instead, it threw out smoke. Smoke rolled out of the new fireplace, filling the room and began spreading through the house. Hastily, the homeowner doused the fire.

Then, sputteringly mad, he went looking for Scrappy.

"That new fireplace and chimney you built for me don't work," he shouted. "I just started a fire. All the smoke comes back out in the room. Your chimney don't draw. You gotta come and fix it."

"You pay me the money you owe me for that job and I'll come and fix it," Scrappy countered.

The homeowner counted out the right amount of cash into Scrappy's hands. "Now come on and fix it before that smoke ruins the rest of my house," he pleaded.

Scrappy positioned a ladder and climbed to the roof, holding an ordinary brick in one hand. He leaned over the open top of the chimney, suspended the brick in the center of the opening, then released it.

From below came the crash of shattering glass.

In the fireplace, he retrieved the brick and the larger pieces of a window-sized pane of glass which he had installed across the chimney brickwork months earlier.

"Now, your fireplace will work," he nodded to the amazed homeowner.

Another man engaged Scrappy to dig a drain ditch across his yard to channel all his waste water from the kitchen out to the side ditch at the street. It took three days of arduous pick-and-shovel work to dig the ditch, install the drain pipe, make the connections and cover up everything. Finished. Scrappy went to collect his money.

But the homeowner evaded. He didn't have any extra money right then. Come back in a few days. Every few days Scrappy stopped by for his money, but some excuse always greeted him. No payment materialized.

One day, the frantic homeowner looked him up.

"That sink drain you fixed ain't working no more. The water's backing up. The sink's overflowing. It's spilling out on the floor. A real mess. We can't stand it. Come back and fix it."

"The only thing wrong is the money you owe me," Scrappy replied. "You pay me the money you owe me for that job and your sink will start working again."

Hastily, the man produced the money.

Back at the worksite, Scrappy removed a few shovelfuls of dirt over the drainpipe near the house. He lifted out a small sandbag which had completely blocked the drain, this sandbag having been installed during his initial work at the site.

The sink drain worked perfectly from then on.

THE MAN WHO JERKED

The reason they called him "Jerky" was obvious. He jerked. Automatically, involuntarily, uncontrollably. He couldn't help jerking, just like you can't help breathing, or sneezing or eating when hunger pangs make your stomach growl.

Say you've got the hiccups. Magnify that ten times. Your whole body would jerk. Your head would bob. Your shoulders would hunch and your arms would balloon outward. Maybe your eyes would bulge, your mouth pop open and your feet tilt you backward a bit.

That's the way it was with Jerky. He jerked every few seconds.

Nature had programmed him that way. Nobody knew why. Nobody cared. Why do some individuals have an extra finger or toe? An extra tooth, different colored eyes, a lisp in their voice or a permanent frown creased in their forehead? Jerky had jerked as long as anyone could remember. Nobody knew his real name anymore—just Jerky. Middle-aged and medium-sized, though a bit on the thin side, Jerky had a bony face punctuated by two dark eyes, which conveyed a permanent expression of surprise at his jerking; as if the jerking annoyed him as much as anyone.

Nothing ever surfaced concerning his background or ancestry. No family, no relatives, not even close friends. He lived by himself in a tumbledown shack in the Uwharrie village and existed by gardening, handouts, oddjobbing for neighbors and helping some of the farmers. He loved going to church and listening to the organ playing and the choir singing beloved old hymns. Seldom did he miss an opportunity to hear music and singing.

Then, Jerky got religion and it changed his life forever.

It happened one hot August night during a revival at the little community church.

The preacher ended his sermon with a dramatic altar call. The organ pleaded with you. The choir's message touched deep emotions. Jerky didn't walk down to the altar, he ran and clutched the preacher and shouted his desire to be a better Christian and to help his fellowman more. That's all it took. The preacher and congregation and the community embraced him.

From then on, all Jerky wanted to do was preach. Not work, just preach. A calling for which he was totally unprepared.

He roamed all over the Uwharries and beyond looking for places to preach. When he found a receptive place, he stayed there and preached as long as the people would tolerate him, which ranged from a few days to a few months. Some people locked their doors to get rid of him. Others had to physically pick him up and throw him off the premises.

Others escorted him to a new locality which needed a preacher. Most of his time was spent, not preaching, but trying to find a place to preach on a regular basis. Such a place proved elusive.

Jerky's voice jerked along with his body. This is what always got him in trouble. People just couldn't long stand seeing his body jerk and hearing his voice jerk at the same time. Every few words or after a short sentence or two, his voice interrupted itself with an explosive jerk, much worse than a loud hiccup, which destroyed composure as well as continuity. Often the physical jerk and the vocal jerk occurred simultaneously with disastrous consequences. When this happened, one person compared him to a small volcano noisily trying to erupt. Initially, listeners were fascinated with his double jerking. But after a few minutes, it became tiresome, offensive and intolerable. His audiences soon disappeared.

With such a devastating handicap, most individuals would give up and find some other line of work to pursue. Not Jerky. He persisted. Mostly illiterate and totally lacking in formal training, he persisted. No one doubted his sincerity. On the other hand, no one, much less a congregation could long endure his pronounced eccentricity. One free meal or one night's lodging became a lucky day for him.

It took years, but, finally, Jerky found a home of sorts.

Old Salvation Primitive Baptist Church took him in on a trial basis.

Practically lost in the obscurity of the Uwharrie wilderness, Old Salvation had been on the brink of collapse for a decade. Only a handful attended its irregular services, occurring only when a maverick itinerant so-called preacher could be persuaded to come. Nobody could remember the last legitimate pastor on a regular basis.

Jerky agreed to preach once a week or more, officiate at funerals and weddings, and help maintain the premises for one-half the money put in the collection plate, plus handouts. Also, he could improvise living quarters for himself in one corner of the decaying frame structure. The next year or so became the happiest period in Jerky's preaching life. Not so for the congregation. The people despised him. Even children recoiled at his jerkiness. No rapport could be established with anyone. Resentment flared. Clashes came frequently. Still, Jerky persisted.

One handed-down comment from a church elder summed it up:

"His preaching weren't worth a cuss. Just a bunch of rambling and spoutin' off. Didn't inspire nobody. Didn't know how to. No points in his mouthing. All us older folks got discouraged with him pretty quick. A few new people did come to church. But not to hear 'im preach. They just came to see and witness that spectacle of him jerking all over the place. That's what brought 'em. Sorta like a circus or sideshow freak. Some of the new people came back later and brought their friends to see this act. Some of 'em kept on doing so for weeks. That's all that kept the church going. But Jerky thought it wuz his preaching that brought 'em, so he kept going and hopin'. Big nuisance. We put up with it long as we could. He wouldn't leave. So we had to do something."

The menfolk got together for a strategy session.

They discussed ways of getting rid of their undesirable pastor.

What could they do? Lock the church door? Cut his pay and reduce the handouts? Find him another church or community far away to go to? One man suggested they blindfold Jerky, hogtie him, gag him if necessary, then transport him by mule and wagon ten miles down in the sandhills or somewhere and dump him and his few belongings out beside a lonesome road at night.

Another suggestion—make him work hard filling up a big deep hole outside one corner of the church. Years ago some enthusiastic members decided the church needed a well to provide fresh water for the churchgoers, especially important at Big Meetings, revivals and protracted services. A water-witcher used his divining rod to pinpoint the best location, just a few feet from the church, outside a pulpit window. They dug and dug. At forty feet and no sign of water, they ran into impenetrable solid granite bedrock and had to give up. All the excavated material was piled around the top of the yawning hole to reduce the hazard it posed. Later, a rough fence was erected around three sides of the hole, and the ends fastened to the side wall of the church. As the years passed, saplings grew up in the pile and snakes denned amid the rocks.

No one had the energy or inclination to refill the hole. If they assigned this formidable task to Jerky as an ultimatum, would he balk and leave?

Nature intervened before they could approach Jerky with this stratagem.

It happened at a nighttime service, better attended than usual. Jerky prattled away in the pulpit, prancing around and waving his arms, making sucking and whistling noises when the jerkiness interfered with his vocal chords. Adults in the congregation stared at him with amusement. Children snickered. A few people stomped their feet. Others clapped their hands and imitated Jerky with exaggerated jerks of their heads and bodies. Others whispered loudly in short, jerky sentences. None of it bothered Jerky.

Abruptly, the wind howled fiercely outside, accompanied by the ominous rumble of thunder. Streaks of lightning split the darkness outside and the dimness inside. The old building creaked. You could almost feel it stretching and heaving. A harder gust of wind slammed into the structure, causing the glowing kerosene lamps hanging from the ceiling to sway and swing. The flame of one lamp snuffed out, bringing a gasp from the congregation. Concerned people stood up and clutched one another. Screaming wind battered harder. The old structure jiggled and shuddered. Windows and doors ripped out of their casement. One section of ceiling and roof caved in. Walls leaned outward, then partially collapsed, bringing more roof debris down inside. Everybody huddled into one corner still intact. Someone said they saw Jerky jump out one of the pulpit windows.

Within a few moments, the cyclone had spent its fury and moved on, leaving havoc behind.

The church was flattened, except for the one corner and small section of overhanging roof which saved all the people. Someone said this corner fell as soon as the people vacated it. Buggies and wagons were overturned and wrecked. Mules and horses stampeded. Most of the people had to walk home. During the storm, the kerosene lamps had fallen into dry timbers, starting fires which consumed most of the church wreckage. A few men remained on the premises to subdue the fire and to check for any missing people.

What happened to Jerky? Officially, nobody knows for sure. But speculation continues almost to this day. One theory dominates.

When Jerky jumped out the pulpit window, he landed practically on the brink of the yawning hole. Unbalanced and fearful in the darkness, he staggered backward into the hole and probably fell all the way to the bottom, which rendered him unconscious. Tree limbs, splintered boards and debris from the demolished church fell in on top of him, practically filling the hole. If the men who stayed behind heard any moaning, groaning or pleading from a subterranean source, they never told about it.

Next morning, dozens of community people came to look upon the scattered pile of rubble, which is all that remained of the church. Before the fire got a good start, the wind blew random boards and debris into the trees for half a mile. An old oak tree had fallen into the wreckage and the fire consumed most of it. A few keepsakes were salvaged.

Inquiries were made about Jerky's whereabouts. But nobody knew. Searches were made in the adjoining woods to no avail.

The men decided to finish filling up the hole using the rubble from the demolished church. This they did with shovels, wheelbarrows and mule-drawn scoops, depositing the excess in ravines in the edge of the woods. Soon, the entire area, hole and all, was cleared and leveled in case a future group of people wanted to build a new church at this location, which never happened.

Gradually, references to Jerky and his fate faded, with the prevailing opinion being that the storm just blew him away. Anyway, the churchmen had their problem solved with a bonus. Not only did they get rid of Jerky, but they got rid of a deteriorating church as well. Nobody questioned the methodology. The storm did it all.

Ever since, there have been reports of babbling ghosts in the Uwharries. These ghosts have an easily discernible jerk to their countenance, reminiscent of a colorful preacher of long ago who labored dedicatedly under a severe handicap. Also, there are reports of the earth trembling and shaking, comparable to minor earthquake tremors, which Uwharrians attribute to the ghost of ol' Jerky who persists in trying to preach despite his jerkiness. So the ghost who approaches you might prefer preaching to you instead of scaring you.

And if you listen closely at a certain location, folks claim you can hear the plaintive, staccato, voice of ol' Jerky's ghost pleading for release from its deep subterranean grave.

THE DISCIPLINARIAN

Here's another Uwharrie personality I never got to meet personally. Yet, I can identify with him quite well.

Today's teachers and educators who face discipline problems might want to consider a technique used by an early educator in central North Carolina's Uwharrie Mountains.

He maintained strict discipline in his classroom and on his school premises. His identity has faded into the mists, but his legacy of effective discipline lives on in folklore.

This man earned widespread acclaim, albeit by word of mouth, because his students excelled. They were notably superior to students from other comparable schools in the region. Fellow educators pressed this teacher to reveal his secret.

But he chose not to divulge his discipline methods, other than to tell his questioners that his M.O. was practical, convenient and worked well, which was obvious.

So envious were some of his contemporaries that they visited his school and observed during the long classroom day. Uniformly they were disappointed. No significant discipline problem arose, at least not big enough to bring his secret weapon into play.

One such visiting teacher allegedly reported on his visit: "The students were quiet and orderly, very attentive, alert and eager and responsive. They were neat, they were respectful, they were determined to please their teacher. How does he do it? We must find out."

But the successful disciplinarian was reluctant to talk about this technique. Not until old age and ill health forced retirement near the end of his life did he tell how he did it.

And then his secret turned out to be so simple that people who heard it laughed uproariously. Not at the efficacy of his method for it really worked for a few other teachers who subsequently tried it, but at the ludicrousness of it.

So if today's teachers have the inclination and the, ah, capacity, they may want to take a closer look at how this early Uwharrian educator handled his discipline problems with such precision, and do likewise.

All this happened scores of years ago when community schools were just that, indeed. Most were crudely built one-room, one-teacher structures to which students walked from miles around to attend classes for a few months out of the year, usually in winter. Drinking water was obtained in buckets from a natural spring down the hill. Bathroom facilities were equally primitive. Students were utilized in bringing in firewood for the wood-burning heater inside.

Most always students brought their own individual lunches with them from home, usually in a brown paper bag, lard bucket or shoebox. These lunch containers were placed in plain view on a shelf until lunchtime, with no sneaking and snacking allowed.

The teacher did everything. In addition to teaching grades K-8 and students ages five through 16 or 17, the lone teacher served as principal, secretary, coach, custodian, counselor, groundskeeper, fire-builder, bell ringer, guardian and nurse. In such an environment, those without regimentation, authoritative command and unrelenting leadership stamina made no progress.

Throughout his long teaching career, our Uwharrie educator remained healthy and robust. He is remembered as well over six feet tall and big-bodied. As his career and his life faded simultaneously, he is said to have described to a friend his discipline secret somewhat as follows:

"Every time a new student comes to the school, I set him down and we have a talk. A straight talk. No nonsense. Eyeball to eyeball. He knows I mean business. He's here to learn, not to loaf. I'm seeing to it that he does learn. He answers to nobody but me while he's at my school. I'm his everything.

"By the time we get through talking, he knows exactly what he can do and what he can't do at this school. I mean exactly, too. He knows the consequences if he deviates. Every now and then I demonstrate what these consequences are, just for good measure, just to remind them, just to keep them in line.

"I give them one chance and one chance only. And they know this well. They can misbehave and break the rules one time. But one time only—and that's it. If they ever misbehave and break the rules again, **I eat their lunch!**"

LANKY DAN THE SHELTER MAN

"Pile out and jaw a-while," Lanky Dan greeted me as I parked my pickup abreast of a bench outside his decrepit shop where he repaired some mule harness. Never before had I been invited to "pile-out". As I vacated my pickup and approached him, I sensed a memorable encounter.

He tossed aside the harness and stood, his body tall and lanky. Plenty of sinew in that wiry body, I knew. Also in the gnarled but nimble hand that gripped mine in greeting. A perennial grin of amusement lightened his sunburned face.

"They call you Lanky Dan," I said. "How come?"

"Durned if I know," he chuckled. "I guess 'cause I'm lanky. 'An Dan 'cause I'm dandy." He laughed. "'Course, they call me other things, too, some not as purty."

"I'll bet I know one other name they call you," I ventured. He nodded. "The shelter feller."

"That's why I came to see you," I said, "to find out if it's true, what they say about you building shelters in the woods."

"Yep, reckon it is," he responded. "'Course they tell things about me and the shelters that ain't so."

"I'd like to see you build one," I said. He nodded. He liked to nod his head.

"Oaky-do. Build one about every day or so. Done an' done one this mornin'. But we can do another 'un."

He turned and motioned all around him. Woods closed in every direction. "Which way you wanna go? I can do it anywheres there's woods. You pick the way you wanna go."

"Okay, let's go over here," I said, pointing toward a wooded rise.

A few hundred yards into the thick woods he paused, then transformed into flurry motion. His hands, feet and body merged into harmonious synchronization. You could tell he had done this before. He grabbed a few arm-sized dead limbs and dropped them against a tree trunk, then fitted smaller limbs and branches in a patchwork mesh across the angled structure. He broke off several pine boughs and branches, placing these strategically. Next he piled on all the forest floor litter he could find, dead leaves, pine needles, bark, hulls, vines, weeds and sticks.

Not more than a few minutes had passed until he called: "Come look."

I knelt at one open side and looked at his handiwork.

Under there was enough room for at least two people to sit or lie prone and probably keep dry in a rainstorm. Big enough for sleeping bags, too. I marveled at the rapidity of its construction and the cleverness of its alleged waterproof design. I visualized people getting lost in the woods and needing such a temporary structure to use overnight. Wonder if I could build one? Could anybody build one under dire circumstances? Using only natural materials found in the woods?

For the first time I noticed a sheathed hatchet attached to Lanky Dan's belt.

But I had not seen him use it. I asked about it.

"Na, don't use it much. I try to get by without using it. But sometimes I hafta use it to keep from walking so far to find what I need."

"Do you or your family or friends ever use these shelters?" I asked.

"Na, hardly ever. Maybe once in a long time, maybe in cold weather. Once, a cold rain started just as I got finished and I dived under there and stayed till it quit raining."

Do animals use the shelters?"

"Na, animals won't use 'em."

How about when it snows?

"Na, not even then."

Are the lean-to shelters used for anything else? He shook his head.

"Well, what do you do with the shelter once you finish building it?"

"Watch!"

He hauled off and started kicking and slinging the shelter components helterskelter. I dodged behind a tree and watched. In a minute, he had kicked and flung all the material in a random arc away from the site, leaving little sign of the picturesque structure of a moment ago. Practically every item he had used re-absorbed itself into the mast and undergrowth.

It took me an instant to integrate what I had witnessed. A substantial, sustainable lean-to shelter built in ten minutes or so, then destroyed in one. Why? Yes, why?

"I like to leave Mother Nature back like I found it," he said in response to my puzzled expression."

Then, he added: "I don't want to use 'em, all I wanna do it build 'em."

"How long you been building shelters like this in the woods?"

"'Bout all my life," he said. He studied my face as if debating whether to continue. The odds that day favored me. We found a log to sit on. His voice mellowed and twanged.

"'Bout seven, yeah, I was seven. Long, long time ago. Pa and me walked to Grandpa's house. Must be eight-ten miles. Cold January day. Dark clouds. Icy wind. We started back home late in the day. Just footpaths and trails through the woods most of the way. Got dark. Real dark. Then it started snowin'. Thick, heavy snow. Blankets o' snow. Covered everything. Pa lost his bearings. We was lost. We couldn't been more'n half away back. It looked like it would snow all night and we'd freeze to death. Pa didn't know which way to go, but he did know what to do.

"He found a likely place under some low trees. We raked back the snow. We mounded up a big pile of dead leaves and pine needles and litter. Then Pa found some dead limbs to prop up against the tree. He crossed them with smaller limbs and branches, using lots of pine boughs and evergreens. Then, he piled on everything he could find to make it thick. He propped a log against the middle to hold it in place. He found a couple of old stumps to stop up the opening at one end. He done a good job. It kept the snow out and most of the wind.

"We got inside and closed the opening behind us. Then we rooted down under that big pile of leaves an' needles an' litter and kept it over us all night. I listened to the wind a-moaning, the shelter creaking and them snowflakes prattlin' down and I wondered if we'd be alive the next morning. Pa held me close and I went to sleep listening to his heartbeat. But before I went to sleep, and other times when I woke up, I heard Pa a-prayin'. His voice went right into my ear. He prayed to God to spare our lives, to let us live through this terrible night. And God answered his prayer, too, or I wouldn't be here.

"Next morning, the sun shone bright. We dug ourselves outta that shelter. Pa was stiff and sore. I was cold and hungry. He hugged me. He looked way up in the trees heavy with snow and he thanked God for sparing our lives. As we left, I looked long at that shelter for I knew it had saved our lives. I knew I could build some like it. And I have. I've been building 'em ever since. I don't care if they're never used. I intend to keep building 'em long as I live. Everybody who walks in the big woods ought to know how to build a shelter. Before we got outta sight, Pa stopped and turned and saluted that shelter. He didn't say why. I didn't' ask. I do that myself sometimes now. I'll stop and salute before I kick 'em down."

As we walked out of the woods, Lanky Dan stopped and looked at me.

"I won't ever build skyscrapers in Atlanta," he said, "but I'll build shelters here in the big woods."

Back in his yard, I sensed a change in his countenance. He even looked different. Much less enigmatic. A lot more friendly. A glow blossomed in his face.

He seemed genuinely glad that my visit gave him a chance to talk about his preoccupation with the shelters. When we parted, his warm handshake proved it.

He leaned into the window of my pickup, his face beaming.

"If ever you're back this way, pile out and we'll chat some more."

AUNT HATTIE

Aunt Hattie was one of these joyous people who didn't tolerate any lethargy or even mild depression in her presence. Verbally, bodily she pounced on anything negative and flailed it unmercifully as she would a slimy creature, forcing it back into its lair in the deep lagoon. Freddie, our son, learned a lot from Aunt Hattie during her brief visit with us one summer.

Medium-sized with a strong chin and flashy eyes under her white hair, Aunt Hattie lived with her children in Arizona and California and only occasionally had the opportunity to visit back home with relatives in her native Uwharries. In our family clan, her visits took on an aura of intrigue and festivity associated with a formal visit by the Pope or the President. All of us tried to contact Aunt Hattie and invite her into our homes as often as we could during her infrequent visits which never lasted more than a few weeks.

When Aunt Hattie talked, the rest of us just listened and laughed.

On her last visit in our home—she sensed it was the last through that cosmic computer which some venerable elderly people have built into their longevity systems—she shared with us intimately, carefully engineering her stories for calculated effect. Freddie learned much about public speaking, story telling and the subtleties of dramatic enunciation from our sessions in the cool of the evening on our front porch overlooking central

North Carolina's Uwharrie Mountains, through which Aunt Hattie had rambled as a girl.

"We had such fun over there at the Narrows on the Yadkin River," she said, nostalgically, "picnicking, sightseeing, fishing, hiking, and playing games. Easter Sunday and Monday used to be times when everyone for miles around went to the Narrows for the day. Courting couples called the outing to the Narrows the highlight of the year. Some of them would flirt and carry on outrageously. I know, because I was one of them. Parents and elders couldn't control you too closely, you know, once you disappeared amongst all those big boulders and trees and bushes all over the hillsides along the river. Why, I could tell you some X-rated stories about some of the situations I ran up on and saw with my own eyes, but it wouldn't do any good to call names even though it's been over fifty years ago. At least one of the hussies is still living today and she'd flog me if I was to say something scandalous and besmirch her character.

"Some of the men would build a hot fire down close to the river and they'd fry fish in a big ol' sizzlin' hot skillet just about as fast as they were caught from the river. You could go eat fish anytime the whole day long. The young men kept the fire going all Saturday and Sunday nights during Easter weekend, and they'd sit up most of the night fishing and drinking and eating and talking about women. A natural spring on the mountainside there furnished good, cold spring water. Of course, some of the girls brought lemonade. And we had coffee and tea. Always there was a little moonshine snuck away on the hill somewheres and many of the men took a dram. Girls taking a drink of moonshine back then was almost unheard of, but I knew one or two who did it. You know, I've almost forgotten how Stanly County moon-shine tastes it's been so long.

"Moonshine reminds me of Tom Marks, King of the Nar-rows, who made moonshine for years around that section of the county. He was caught by the revenuers several times, but he never did serve any time. His moonshine was the best in the hills, so I've heard all the men folks say. He operated on both sides of the river, that's why officers had such difficulty catching him. Once they had him handcuffed and were bringing him in, but they had to get across the river. He offered to paddle them across in a homemade bateau. Out about mid-river, he turned the bateau over and threw everyone out. Tom disappeared in the water and the officers never saw him again that day.

"Another time the two officers surprised him at his still and caught him fair and square. He asked them to let him go by his home and change clothes before going on to jail in Albemarle and they agreed. Once inside his home he asked his wife to go with him in a back room and help him find some clothes, while the officers waited in the main part of the house. Tom said to his wife in a loud voice: 'Honey, how about taking the bucket and going down to the spring and getting a fresh bucket of water so I can enjoy one last drink of good ol' cold spring water before I have to go set in that stinking jail in town, will you?' 'I'll be glad to,' she said.

"Soon a figure in a long dress, head swathed in a wrap-around sun bonnet, walked across the main room past the officers, out on the porch, got a wooden water bucket off the shelf and walked down the path toward the spring. Meantime, sounds continued coming from the back room like someone was changing clothes. Minutes passed. Finally the officers decided it was time they were checking to see why it was taking Tom Marks so long to change clothes. They peeked inside the back room. There sat a grinning woman. Only then did they realize they had been tricked! The person in a long dress and sun bonnet who walked out to go get a bucket of water had been none other than Tom Marks himself. By now he was long gone in his favorite woods where no man could catch him on the run.

"Once more Tom Marks had given the law the slip. He was good at doing that.

"There used to be a large flat rock close to the river which you could see from up on the hills. People used to come for miles away to see that rock. Most unusual rock. They say it'd put on a show sometimes. Darndest thing you ever saw a rock do. Every time that rock heard a rooster crow, it would flip over, completely change positions. People came from everywhere in hopes of catching that rock flipping. They'd even bring roosters with them and make 'em crow. That rock still might be performing if you all want to go look for it. Be worth your time. One thing's sure, now, every time that big rock hears a rooster crow, it'll flip. You can count on it.

"Yep, a lot of lives were made gladder by things that happened around those Narrows of the Yadkin River...."

She fell silent for awhile, pensive, moody. Then she brightened.

"Preachers used to hold services there at the Narrows in that Natural Cathedral of God's beauty. And they had baptizings in the river, too....

"Preachers...m-mmm...did I tell you about the time I tricked one of our young, just-getting-started preachers out in Arizona? Just a young fellow, right out of the seminary, probably young enough to be my grandson. Good kid. Sharp, friendly, smiled a lot, good personality. He wanted to help everybody. He called me 'Aunt Hattie' like everybody else did. I figured I could pull this one on him. It seldom fails. Any good-little-old-lady like me can foist it off on an unsuspecting pastor fresh out of the hall of academy.

"'Pastor Jones', I said to him one Sunday after services, 'that was a fine sermon which required a lot of Biblical background and knowledge.' Reminds me of a question I've had for years. Maybe you can help me with it. Who was the father of Zebedee's sons? I asked the question real seriously and expectantly. He looked puzzled. 'The father of Zebedee's sons?' he repeated. 'Offhand I don't know, Aunt Hattie, but I'll do some research and find out for you okay?' I told him okay, to let me know when he found out. But he never did tell me. When he realized what a joke I was pulling on him, he became so self conscious he probably decided to just let it ride and never mention it again. So I did the same; I never mentioned it to him either. Though there were times when we'd happen to glance at each other and grin like we shared a secret. I guess I ought to be ashamed of my mean self for pestering a poor innocent, young preacher like that."

Aunt Hattie died like she wanted—quickly ("let's get it over with"), no burden on anyone—and was buried back in her beloved North Carolina. A lot went with her—volumes of local history and lore, a role model matriarch, a whiplash of a woman whose dynamic presence kept everyone in line, and, most of all, a loveable and peppery personality whose absence from our clan will never again be filled in such a memorable way.

Whenever I think nostalgically about Aunt Hattie and melancholy sets in, all that is swept away, as she intended, when I remember her classic good humor, especially the way she put down a young airline reservationist who got uppity with her when she telephoned to find out how much it would cost to fly her body from out West back to North Carolina.

"Body!?" the airline clerk joked. "Dead or alive?"

"Dead," Aunt Hattie retorted. "Mine. Me. My body. I'm not dead yet. I'm not ready to crawl in that box yet. But when I do, I want to be brought back to North Carolina for burial. So how much does it cost to fly a body, a dead body, from Arizona to North Carolina? My body?"

THE ONE-STORY MAN

Jeff Holler was a character with a story to tell. Just one story. And tell it he did. To generations of avid listeners. Just that one story from his own personal experience. He learned how to tell it effectively in a variety of take-offs, approaches and viewpoints. Until he became old and decrepit. Jeff told the story live, on his feet, so he could act out parts of it. He captivated any audience, individual or group; young, old, in-between, male or female, sophisticated, or redneck country buffoons. All were held captive by his enthusiasm. No matter how many times you had heard the story, it always came across fresh and intriguing with ribald hilarity. Somehow the repetition never registered on anyone, though they may have heard this yarn a dozen times. Jeff Holler really had a story to holler about.

It happened back in the mule-and-wagon days when Jeff was thirteen years old and lived on a farm in a remote part of the Uwharries.

The only way to tell his story is to paraphrase it the way he told it.

"Our neighbor, ol' man Tolliver...he musta been eighty or better...stove up and twisted...probably didn't weigh a hunnard pounds...well, he died suddenly one morning. The neighbors come and got 'im ready for buryin'... no undertakers much back then...and I helped the men build a pine box coffin. We lined it with quilts and put in a piller fer his head. All cozy and tight.

"But we weren't gonna bury him here. His daughter...Daphine, I believe they called her...lived ten miles away over in the Birkheads. We were gonna haft to haul the body over there. She wanted the funeral at a little country church close by. Her neighbor men were already digging a grave to bury her father in the family plot at the old homeplace where she lived. My Uncle Pete and his friend, Sam Bussyplat, volunteered to drive the hoss and wagon and body over there. My Ma made me go along with 'em...she said to show our respect for our dearly departed neighbor.

"I didn't want to go, but Ma made me. I was tired out from working in the field, sleepy, too, 'cause the night before we had possum hunted about all night and I didn't get to sleep hardly any. And it's cold...cold as a armful of icicles. Icy wind, a-blowin' through ya, thick clouds overhead like it might snow. Never seen such a cold winter day. I wore my long underwear, two pair o' overalls, two shirts, a heavy sweater and a overall jacket on top. Ma made me wear two pair of thick socks in my brogans and this heavy knitted wool boggan over my head and ears. Mostly I kept my hands in my pockets.

"But I was still cold and getting colder all the time.

"They made me sit in the middle between them on the seat...just a board stretched across the front of the wagon body. The pine box occupied by the dead man, rested on the wagon bed floor behind us. Uncle Pete and Sam mouthed to each other, tried to sing a little and acted crazy. They passed a bottle of moonshine between them, without letting me touch it. Our breaths came out ghostly white. The intense cold didn't seem to bother Uncle Pete's hoss, ol' Bell...he just ate up the rough dirt road.

"We left late in the day and hoped to get to our destination before midnight 'cause a bunch of folks were sittin' up there waitin' on us. The wake would be the rest of that night and the next day an' night. All of us about froze on that wagon seat. Br-rrr, it was cold. The two men said: 'damn, it's cold, too cold to be out here.' I got so freakin' cold I told them I was ready to jump out of the waggin' and trot' back home. Nobody had thought to bring a lap robe to cover our freezing feet and legs. That lighted lantern hanging on the corner of the wagon bed looked warm enough to touch, but it didn't do nothing to warm us up.

"Finally, about halfway, we come to Snook's Place, a run-down sprawling ol' farmhouse right beside the road. I'd heard you could get about anything you wanted at Snook's Place–food, drink, whiskey, poker playing, lodging, even companionship of a sort. We stopped and they tied ol' Bell's lead rope to a hitching post. Uncle Pete and Sam said they were going inside to warm up and get a drink. But they wouldn't let me go in. 'No place for a boy,' they tole me. 'You gotta stay here and guard the body.' They laughed. I begged to go in. But they wouldn't listen. I threatened to leave and run back home if they didn't hurry back out, so we could get going again.

"An' idee hit me.

"Them buzzards weren't coming out anytime soon. I heard hee-hawing laughter from inside. They might be in there for an hour. An' leaving me out here to freeze. Hell, I had to do something. I turned and looked at that coffin. Right beside it lay a big eight-foot-wide roll of tarpaulin that we brought along to cover us with in case of rain or snow or ice falling. Why not...? I jerked open the coffin lid. I got ol' Tolliver's body out. I unrolled a piece of the tarp, put the body under it and smoothed the tarp back in place. The tarp looked no different than before 'cause the body was slight and light. I crawled into that coffin and snugged the lid down tight. I stretched out and put my head on the dead man's piller. Plenty of air gittin' in for me to breathe good. Soon, I was warm and cozy. I relaxed all over. My eyes got heavy and closed.

"The next thing I remember, I came half awake enough to feel the wagon jarring over rough ground. I knew we were moving. I could tell when the wagon went downhill and uphill, when it forded the creek and when the wheels crunched over loose rock. It was so warm and comfortable inside that coffin. I wasn't about to disturb anybody. Anyway, they thought I had left and gone back home. I went back into a sound sleep.

"A jerk woke me up. I felt the coffin moving off the wagon bed. I heard the mumble of voices and the shuffling of feet as the swaying coffin moved toward the house.

"'Damn, ol' man Tolliver musta growed some on the way over here,' Uncle Pete growled. 'Seems like he's heavier now.'

"After more jostling around and angling up steep steps, the coffin entered a lighted room. I could see slivers of light coming through the cracks around the edge of the lid. Musta been several oil lamps in the room. It felt like they sat each end of the coffin down on the seat part of two straight chairs for it did-n't move anymore. Judging from the voices, there musta been a dozen people in the room. Someone invited Uncle Pete and Sam to the kitchen for hot coffee and cake.

"What was I to do? Wide awake now, I pondered it. Start yelling and thumping to be freed from the coffin? Kick the lid off and sit up? Or just start a little faint groanin' and moanin' to shake them up a little?

"Then I heard someone say, 'Well we might as well open the casket so everybody here can see what Daphine's Pa looks like. Preacher, is it okay if we open it up?'

"The preacher gave his okay. I heard steps toward the coffin.

"Right then I let out a kinda wavy moan, a little gurgle and a slight knee bump on the inside wall of the coffin.

"Deathly quiet. No sound or movement. I could almost hear heavy breathing and muscles tensing up. Then somebody spoke.

"Whut was that?"

"Preacher did you hear that?"

"I threw my body weight against one side of the coffin and felt it lurch like it was about to fall off the chairs. At the same time I gave a louder, muttery moany groan.

"Several feminine screams rent the air. Feet scampered back away from the coffin. Someone dropped a tool. From outside the house came the baleful howl of a hound dog.

"Git me outta here, please," I cried in a ghostly voice. "Git me outta here."

"My feet kicked one end of the lid loose. I used my knees and arms to finish poppin' it up and sliding the lid off to one side. Then I sat up, rubbed my eyes and looked around.

"All hell broke loose. I mean it did. Everybody screamed and shouted, gasped and stuttered, stammered and pointed. One woman fainted and fell over on the floor. People shoved each other around in a mad scramble for the doors. Chairs overturned and got kicked a-windin'. In their dash to get out, the fleeing occupants created such a rush of air that it blowed out two lamps, reducing visibility to sinister twilight. One oldster grabbed a shotgun from the corner and started to level it at me and the coffin, but another man grabbed it away. Somebody hollered for the Preacher to come, but he was nowhere to be found.

"I stood up straight in the coffin and stretched, the top of my head brushing the ceiling.

"A few people eased timidly back in the room. More faces peered around the door jambs. Uncle Pete and Sam came back from the kitchen.

"A rush of questions tumbled out in quavering voices.

"'Lawd-a-mighty, whut's happening?'

"'What...who is it?'

"'The devil's done come to rise up and get us ...'

"'That ain't my Pa,' Daphine screeched, throwing her hands up, then covering her eyes. 'Who is it?'

"Only then did I realize that I was a complete stranger to all these people...nobody knowed me except Uncle Pete and Sam and it looked like they were too shocked to speak up. They just stood there, wide-eyed, like they couldn't believe it.

"I stepped over the side of the coffin with one foot on the floor. Everybody moved back. The women moaned. The men spread their arms as if to protect the women from a monster. The oldster found his shotgun again and mumbled. 'I'll shoot 'im, I'll shoot 'im.' Somebody stopped him. Another man had the presence of mind to light the still smoking wicks of the blowed-out lamps. This improved light seemed to calm down everybody a little. But not much.

"Uncle Pete and Sam finally spoke up.

"'This boy is with us...he came with us on the wagon...but we thought he left...went back home...did he open up that coffin and...no...he couldn't have...no...'

"Daphine screamed again. 'So, where's my Pa?' Whut have you done with my Pa?'

"Uncle Pete and Sam got over their jitters and come up and grabbed me by the arms...to convince themselves that I was real, I think. They looked in the empty coffin.

"They leaned closer and rasped in my year. 'Where's the body?'

"I shrugged and looked blank like I didn't know or remember anything about the body.

"They gripped my arms turrible tight and Sam growled in my ear. 'These people are gittin' mighty mad and ornery. They may git mad enough to kill us all if we don't produce that body. Now, tell us, whut did you do with the body?'

"I started to resist, then changed my mind. Every eye in that room drilled me. The old man fiddled around with the shotgun in his trembling hands, the barrel pointed in my direction. Along with me, they'd probably shoot Uncle Pete and Sam, too. If I didn't speak up. If we didn't produce a body. Real quick, too.

"I spoke low so only Uncle Pete and Sam could hear me. 'While you two were inside the Snook's Place, I was plain freezing to death. I took the lid off the coffin and got Tolliver out and put his body under the tarp, then I got in the coffin and fastened the lid down. The body's out there under the tarp in the wagon bed...unless...unless some wild animal has done drug it off by now.'

"They released my arms and hurried outside, saying they'd be right back. Two men in the room followed them. All the rest of them sorta closed in around me to be sure I didn't go anywhere. Daphine kept her dagger eyes on me. She kept mumbling about me taking the place of her dear dead dad and that if they didn't find his body real soon they might use his coffin to bury me alive in, since I liked it so good.

"They brought in the body.

"Uncle Pete and Sam toted it in, one at each end, like toting a log. It appeared to be frozen stiff and solid, with some ice showing around the feet and head. Daphine squalled and tried to mother the frozen body. After they placed the body in the coffin the women brought warm cloths and tried to warm up and smooth up the body and make it look more presentable. Everybody crowded close for a good look.

"Uncle Pete caught my eye and nodded toward the door. We eased out, got in the wagon and headed for home real fast, relieved that we had escaped without any retaliation. On the trip back, they let me huddle under the tarp where I stayed warmer. In the wee hours, we stopped again at Snook's Place, but it was dark and closed up and nobody got to go in. We got back home about daylight. Ma wouldn't let me go to bed and sleep any. She sent me right out in the woods with the others to cut crossties all day long.

"When Ma found out about my part in that coffin deal, she got spittin' mad. She woulda whupped me if she had been strong enough. She tried to anyway. Then, people got to laughing about me and the coffin. They made me tell that story all the rest of my long life an' every time they'd wha-wha in fits o' laughing and slapping their legs.

"Finally, Ma got to laughing about it, too.

"But one thing...lemme tell you fer sure...I never took another ride in a coffin long as I lived!"

OL' BULLET

A hot summer sun blasted down like a fully primed blow-torch when I stopped about 12:30 p.m. at this bleak farmhouse on a lonely Uwharrie road. My old pickup had no air conditioning except for rolled-down windows and a retractable air scoop out front which didn't work well until you reached cruising speed. Cruising speed on this twisty dirt road was a joke. As I parked and got out to greet this farm family lounging on the porch, perspiration bathed my face, ran down my back, even wet the seat of my pants, making me maintain a straightforward approach.

I hurried into the shade at the edge of the porch.

This old weather-blackened house had never been painted. Windows and doors looked like empty eye sockets on the inside wall of the wrap-around porch. From the peak of the wood-shingled roof, lightning rods came down at each corner of the porch and plunged into the ground. Beyond the rain-splashed graveled yard, decorated with a few scraggly oaks, a sagging old barn and a series of outbuildings seemed to stare at you with wondering eyes. I heard a milk cow bellow from the pasture and a mule snort from the barn.

A typical Uwharrie farm family enjoyed the deep shade and stupor of the porch.

I addressed my remarks to the oldest person on the porch, apparently the patriarch of the clan. He looked to be eighty or better. He slouched half asleep in an ancient upholstered chair riddled with slits and perforations. Dirty bare feet protruded from the legs of his tattered overalls. At the other end, his face and head poked out of a threadbare blue shirt. The ends of a wiry handlebar mustache twiddled as he snored. Sweaty gray hair crowned him. Nearby sat a younger couple, one of them probably his offspring. Elsewhere on the porch lounged four children, ranging from a strapping teenage boy to a girl aged four or five. All appeared to be succumbing to the midday torpor.

"My name's Morgan," I ventured. "I'm from Albemarle. I'm doing research. I stop and talk to people about the old days...."

His eyes fluttered open once, then closed. His gnarled hand raised in a futile gesture, then dropped in his lap. A snore told me he had not even acknowledged my presence.

The younger couple woke up enough to tell me: "You'll have to talk a little louder to him," pointing to their ears.

I leaned toward him and repeated my message a little louder.

His eyes jerked open, then closed, then opened and closed again. His body quivered slightly, then he raised his head, his eyes open enough to focus on me.

"Huh?" was all he said.

I repeated my words, adding that I was interested in hearing any tales about the old days that he and his family might remember.

He looked at me hard, then lowered his head. His voice invoked visions of mellow yellow apples.

"Aw, now's not the time. We're tarred out. We worked all mornin' in that hot field. We jist et dinner. We got to lay around and rest a while fore we git back outten that hot field."

He promptly went back to sleep.

I stood there uncertain as to what I should do, thinking maybe I should leave. I turned and started to walk away when his voice stopped me.

"Aw, come on up on the porch and join us. Out on a road like this you can't be in a big hurry. Come on up on the porch and help us rest a while."

Why not? The shade did look inviting. The old man had already closed his eyes again.

I walked to the set of wooden steps leading to the waist-high porch floor. There I stopped again. Something blocked my way.

Lying there stretched all the way length-wise along the middle step was a huge brownish-blackish hound dog getting in his equal part of the noontime siesta. His bristly nose inched off one end of the step; the end of his tail and his hind feet off the other end. The line of advancing sunshine and receding shade inched ever closer to him. Oblivious to everything, he lay there softly snoring.

Should I try to step over him? I hesitated.

The old man woke up enough to note my predicament. He got up stiffly, careened to the steps, took his bare foot and toed the old hound off the steps. The old dog looked remarkably like ol' Bullet who sometimes appears in the Snuffy Smith comic strip in the Sunday funnies. Limp and gawky, ol' Bullet sorta poured off the end of the step and piled up on the ground below, mostly in the hot sunshine. Probably without even waking. The old man reclaimed his chair.

I ascended the steps, then stopped. Another problem. All the seats were taken. I could see no place to sit down. The four children and three adults occupied all the sitting and reclining positions.

Again, the old man rallied. His eyes opened. He jerked upright without leaving the chair.

"Aw, jest set down on the edge of the porch and dangle yer feet," he suggested, promptly retreating into slumber-land.

I sat down on the edge of the porch and dangled my feet. Then, I discovered a support post to one side. So, I leaned my back against the post and spread my legs and feet out flat parallel to the edge of the porch floor. Much more comfortable this way. Soon, I felt myself succumbing to the apathy of the porch atmosphere—soft snoring, heat, fetish air, houseflies loitering around, roof shingles faintly popping and cracking under the intense heat. But I roused. I had to. I couldn't sit there and sleep for an hour with a family I had come to interview.

I shrugged to my senses. I had to make at least one more attempt. I spoke loud enough for everyone to hear.

"I'd like to hear about any old tales—haunted houses, witch women casting spells, mysterious lights and noises at night, anything strange and unusual...anybody remember anything like this?"

No response. Nobody batted an eye. It was as if no one heard me.

Heck! I might as well leave, I began telling myself. No use marking time here with a comatose family and becoming addicted myself. I hunched up one knee, ready to rise and go. But then I stopped. Right then something special happened in my favor.

Evidently, the hot sun got too hot for ol' Bullet for he slowly squirmed to his feet and uttered a low and mournful howl like he was in distress and expected someone to help him. He executed a magnificent stretch—long, scrawny legs and tail, huge floppy ears, big soulful eyes appealing for a handout, sharp whiskers jutting from his snout. He turned around a couple of times, then ambled up the steps onto the porch where he looked both ways, then pattered down the floor and stopped beside me, his breath worse than a billygoat's. He knew I was a stranger and he started sizing me up.

I've been sniffed at before, but never like ol' Bullet sniffed me. His big head came all around me everywhere, his nose sniffing and snorting. He inspected my back, front, sides, legs and feet. He stopped and stared at me, eyeball to eyeball. He inspected some more, than grunted and snorted, his breath stiffling. He turned around twice, then looked long at me. Then he flopped on the floor alongside my legs and placed his hulky head across my legs at the knees. Using my legs as his pillow, he promptly went back to sleep. I heard him snoring.

While ol' Bullet was getting settled, I glanced around at the other human beings on the porch. Every human eye on the porch—all the children and the adults—watched the hound dog perform his routine. Watched him closely, too. They accounted for his every move. I wondered why this close scrutiny?

I didn't especially like the old dog's smelly head across my legs, but instinct told me not to object. I rubbed the top of his head and fiddled with his ears a bit. All the family members were still watching.

Instinct told me to press my case once more, then if I did not get any favorable response, to leave.

Again I told them I was collecting folklore, driving along old country roads and stopping and talking with farm people, mostly older people, and asking them about the old days. Did they remember any interesting tales from their forebears about what happened long ago? Ghosts, witches, haunted houses and places, unsolved murders, strange lights and sounds, invisible visitors, unaccountable turmoil and unrest?

Right then and there, a strange thing happened to me. These drowsy folks came wide awake and began talking, after having ignored my earlier appeals.

And, boy, did they talk! I struggled with my mental note taking.

Eager to talk, the old man jumped out of his chair, hustled over and sat down on the edge of the porch beside me and dangled his feet. He told me about a natural haunted spring of water where slaves had lynched their cruel master and where the ghosts of both the slaves and their master can now be seen coming out of the spring and hovering around; about a railroad ghost, about an audible but invisible team of horses pulling a wheel-crunching wagon along an old road, about fireballs shooting out of an abandoned house, about squeaky trees beside the road that would squeak only when certain people passed, about a witch woman who turned herself into a hog, about the time when it rained tiny frogs.

The younger couple reminded him of other tales they had heard him tell, which he related to me. So did the children.

"Grandpa, tell him about old Mister Dirksen over on the teapot road," the boy suggested. "An', maybe that old lady down yonder that they used to call a witch."

So, I got leads for interviews with at least two more elderly people in the community with entryways into the past.

All in all, I got more material—more quality and variety—from this one family at this one stop than at any other one stop during all my years of such researching.

Practically all this material has been utilized in the ghost story/folklore books I've written. The way this material originated sticks in my memory as a unique example of playing-it-by-the-ear country people interviewing which has never been equaled in my experience.

I'm sure ol' Bullet changed the family's mind. After they watched ol' Bullet inspect me, check me out and approve of me, they figured that was good enough for them; that they could accept me and talk to me upon his recommendation.

It's the first and only time I ever got what I wanted after being endorsed by an old hound dog.

THE PREPETUAL MOTION MAN

Often when I cross the highway bridge over big Lake Tillery, linking Stanly and Montgomery Counties, my mind flashes up a printout of a venerable old gentleman inventor who proposed utilizing this lake in experiments to develop his grandiose idea for a perpetual motion machine.

Although he dreamed and fantasized about it all his adult life, he never lived to see his idea developed beyond the rudimentary stage.

Percy Covington, who lived in nearby Mt. Gilead, remains one of the most memorable of the colorful characters I met during my long years of research in the Uwharries. I met and talked with him only a few times in the late 1940s and early 1950s. He stood beside the street in front of his home on the outskirts of the small town.

There he waved and greeted passersby, some of whom stopped for a chat with this dignified man usually dressed in formal wear, including a necktie. Middle-aged then, his demeanor matched his attire. He talked with erudition and enthusiasm, indicating an academic, or at least a well-read background.

Covington wanted to find a sympathetic, knowledgeable person to collaborate with him, especially to provide funds to finance his experiments.

While his inventive mind produced minor improvements—a way to conserve water in flushing toilets, a no-stick pan for baking, a better mousetrap, a soap drain/holder and other tabletop models in various stages of development–his major interest was perpetual motion. Obsessed with this idea and convinced of its reality, he spent most of his time theorizing, diagramming and talking about it to anyone who would listen. However, few people ever shared his passion. Others considered him a nuisance.

His basic idea for perpetual motion was continuously sloshing water.

He called it his slosh tank. He described it somewhat as follows.

Picture in your mind a traditional shoebox, or a rectangular container several times longer than it is wide. Magnify it to manageable proportions. Using a swivel device, attach its bottom at the exact midway point to a log or a rigid horizontal pipe, so that each end can go up and down freely like a seesaw. Perfect balance with each half the same weight is crucial.

Now fill the low end of the tank with water, all it will hold. Force it upward, so the water will begin running toward the empty end of the tank. This starts the back-and forth sloshing motion. Each end of the tank is designed with a large superstructure, a fan-shaped curved panel which re-directs the surge of water back the way it came. Also, a spongy base for the water-filled heavy end of the tank to strike at its maximum low point would provide some springy uplift. Some elastic bungy-type cables could help pull or push each end at the proper time, too.

Covington envisioned a drive shaft attached at the swivel point at right angles to the tank. Each half of the sloshing cycle would turn the shaft. This constant movement could be harnessed for energy to perform all kinds of work. He said, once started, this sloshing cycle would provide a reliable source of power requiring little maintenance.

He admitted there were bugs and unforeseen problems in his proposal, but these could be solved and ironed out as experimentation proceeded on a gradually expanding scale.

One basic flaw in his vision was the lack of professional evaluation. He probably never succeeded in getting a recognized scientist or engineer to come and look over his simple models and his paperwork theorizing.

Another flaw that he talked about was water replenishment. Water in the tank would be lost by sloshing out and, also, by evaporation. This escaping water would have to be replaced constantly, from a readily available source.

Here's where Lake Tillery enters the picture, not only as the water replenishment source, but as the location for the gargantuan working and energy-producing perpetual motion machine that Covington had in mind—a colossal contraption that utilized thousands of tons of rushing water every cycle.

He described it in generalized, but amazing terms:

His slosh tank would be two miles long and half a mile wide, situated on the biggest, widest part of Lake Tillery, consistent with its natural downstream flow. The tank, at its pivot point, and related structures, possibly a control building, could be installed on support pillars from the bottom of the lake. He said energy produced here by harnessing the perpetual slosh tank motion could be used in a variety of ways. Already, he had envisioned such slosh tanks installed on a number of public waterways and owned and operated by the state, at least licensed and regulated by the state, for the public good.

After all, he said the major raw material used in this process—water—was never consumed, just used.

Only once in our casual conversation did Covington emphasize that he was a man of ideas, so leave the practical applica-
tion part to the professionals. He made it plain that he was
always available for elaboration and consultation.

There were some vague references, never made clear to
me, that Covington had contributed ideas for significant improvement in military weaponry and engine performance during World War II.

My last image of this gentlemanly man of ideas was him
waiting patiently beside the street in front of his home for that
elusive passerby who could help him bring some of his ideas to
fruition.

Invariably when I cross the Jim Garrison Memorial
Bridge over big Lake Tillery, I fancy that I feel the presence of
Percy Covington. I look both ways, upstream and downstream,
to see if there is a ghost of a chance of any implementation of
Covington's grandiose slosh tank perpetual motion machine.

JESS GREENE THE STORY MACHINE

"Yeah, Jess Greene, he's the man you wanna talk to," they all told me when I asked older people about this renowned storyteller from Stanly County. "Yeah, he's the one. Go find 'im."

I went to his last known place of employment. They remembered him fondly. Good man, good worker. But he retired several years ago. Lives out on the edge of town somewhere.

So, I circled the town, stopping and asking. A few people had heard of him; none knew where he lived. It took me days of spare time, stopping and asking. Then more days. Having circled the town twice already, I extended the outer reach of my circle and started back around.

Instinct punched me in my spiritual midriff when I spotted an old man seated in a portable chair in the autumn sunshine outside a mobile home in the edge of some woods.

I had found Jess Greene.

For the next several hours, I sat there spellbound as original stories rolled out of this man as naturally as ocean waves rolling in to the shore. Talking proved therapeutic for him. He needed no prodding.

Products of the good ol' days, his stories are dramatized by benign exaggeration, tinted with genuine country vernacular, spiced with admirable humor and creativity. They were delivered in a voice as homespun and mellowed as a glorious autumn day. Practically all are autobiographical.

As you visualize these tales, try, also, to see the narrator—an affable oldster, balding, slightly paunchy, his owly face crinkling into a constant grin, bringing sparkles to his eyes and voice, plus an almost permanent chuckle accentuating his spontaneous stories.

Ol' George

"I had the best mule anywheres. Man, he wuz a good 'un. Traded fer him over at Marshville. Fresh outta St. Louie. Young and lively and willing to learn. I trained him good that first year. Real good. When I said 'whoa, boy,' he upped and stopped right then. Slammed on his brakes and slid. None of thet fiddlin' around and gradual stuff. He stopped. When I said "Gaddup' boy, he lit out. He minded me better'n any chile you ever seed mind his pappa. He wuz just plain perfect.

"He saved my life, once, ol' George did. Yeah.

"We wuz snakin' logs down in them hills. One place we had to cross this narrow, low, little bridge, across a gorge. Must've been two hundred feet to the water down below. Ol' George was a little skittish about high places, but he managed to git across. All 'cept this one morning. We'd started across when this gang of wild ducks flew up and scared ol' George and he shied to one side and tumbled us off the bridge—me and the big log with him. Here we went a-tumbling head over heels down through the air to certain death when I happent to remember something. I hollered 'whoa!' real loud. Ol' George starts putt-

ing on his brakes and we screeches to a stop just four feet from
that water. Then we climbed on down without getting hurt.
There was all kinds of jagged rocks jest under the surface which
would sure have kilt all of us if I hadn't got ol' George to whoa.

Outpull Anything

"Thet mule outpulled anything in the whole country
around here. Natural boan puller. Didn't git too heavy a load for
'im. He pulled so many heavy loads on muh wagon so many
times, he stretched the wagon tongue so bad I had to cut it off and
shorten it to proper size four different times.

"Trottin'-est mule, too. Trotted him from Albemarle
clean out to home—about 18 miles or so—in two hours oncest.
Long-winded. Liked to go. He'd eat up the road. Outrun a lot of
old Model-Ts back in the T days. See a cloud of dust coming
down a country road and most times you'd know it was ol'
George and the buggy or wagon. Most times he'd be way out in
front of the dust, though, he wuz so fast. Why, lotsa times he'd
run clean out of then shaves and we'd have to turn around and
go back and rehitch to the buggy.

Big Storm

'We wuz plowing one day when this big storm blew up. I
tied ol' George to a tree and lit out fer home. The wind blowed

fierce and the sky wuz full of bresh and dust and stuff. Grandmammy's old rain barrel blowed away from the smokehouse drain and bounced across the field. The lightning struck at it three times and missed every time it wuz cutting' such capers. Then the wind picked up the big, ol', black, heavy cast iron washpot and blowed it completely wrong side out. This didn't bother us none, though, 'cept when grandmammy started stirrin' clothes and the stirrin' stick got tangled up over the three legs and the handles sticking all out inside the washpot. This worried Grandmammy some.

"Out to the barn I heered a terrible struggling and groaning and muttering and I looked around back out there and saw this raw-looking, scary looking thing a-teetering there on the fence. Plumb fearsome. I woulda never knowed, 'cept for the urrking sounds it wuz making. It was granny's old rooster blowed wrong side out. I reached down inside his gullet and grabbed his tail-feathers and jerked him right side out again. Jest in time, too, or he'd been a goner.

"Then I went back to see about ol' George. The wind had blowed him round and round that tree trunk so turrible tight it had 'bout squeezed all the juice outta him. I unwound him and peeled him off the tree. He wuz thin as paper and limp as a dishrag. I spread him out like a blanket on the ground-to die, I thought. But his big eyes pleaded at me desperate fer help. I had to do something. An idee hit me. The wind wuz still blowing some. I worked till I propped his mouth open facing into the wind. Directly along came a big puff of wind right into his mouth and this blowed him back up to normal size again.

Ol' George Bested

"Only one time did I ever see ol' George bested. We wuz cultivatin' corn one hot summer day in the bottom field long by the river. I got so hot I left George in the shade and I shuck off my clothes and went in a-washing to cool off. Thought I'd grabble under the rocks fer fish, too, and mebbe catch me a big catfish fer supper.

"Well, I played around for a while and cooled off, then I got the feeling around under this big rock fer fish. An' I felt one. Giant 'un. Monster. I got one hand in each gill and my hands must've been three feet apart. He coulda swallered me if he had opened his mouth wide. I tugged with all the power in me and I couldn't budge 'im. Then I got this idee.

"I flung on my britches and hurried back to the house and got this big, long, ol' log chain. I threaded this through his gill and mouth and hooked it. The other end I hooked onto ol' George to drag 'im out. He tried and he tried hard. He hunched and he grunted and he heaved and he dug. But he couldn't do no good.

"All of a sudden, ol' George starts mule screaming and a-slippin' backards an' I realize the catfish is headin' fer deep water and draggin' ol' George with him. I barely had time to git muh knife and slash the harness loose and save ol' George from drowning. For years after that, day or night, we could hear that log chain lamming into rocks all up and down the river and we knowed that ol' catfish wuz still on the move. He may still be.

Possum Dog

"Folks allus wondered how I got my possum dog trained so good. She wuz trained away from treein' possums and coons in big trees which we had to climb or use the axe to chop down. None of that. We had her trained so she would tree all of them in bushes and little saplings that we could bend over. It took some doing to get 'er trained this way, but it paid off.

"Finally, I took some of the folks with me and let them see how she worked. Every time a possum or coon started up a big tree, she'd grab 'im and jerk him back. Every time, too. Kept on doing this till the possum finally caught on, then, he's go to a bush or little low sapling and crawl up in it to get away from her. And, of course, she'd let him do this. Then, she'd fire loose in tree barking and baying fer us to come and get 'im. We never even had to take an axe with us into the woods no more. All we had to do wuz bend over little bushes and saplings and drop the possum into the sack. Got up to twenty a night like this.

Rabbit Chaser

"Fanny was the best rabbit dog there's ever been in the Rocky River country. Never lose a rabbit. Nothing took her from the trail. Crazy about runnin' rabbits. Wanted to chase rabbits all time. Sometimes after she'd been running rabbits all night and half the day, I'd have to go outside and ring the dinner bell to get her to come to the house to eat. An' you know what she'd do? When she heard that dinner bell and wuz hungry, she'd stop where she was on the trail and paw out a mark. Then she'd hurry home and eat and go right back to that mark and start up the chase again.

"The woods, fields, hollers and hills around our home wuz full of rabbits. Down in the swamp was an ol' holler popular log which ever rabbit in the country had used at one time or other for denning and nesting purposes or to hole up in when they got scared and the dogs wuz gaining on them. One day I nailed a board over this hole and used chimney soot to blacken a spot on the board exactly where the hole used to be. Then I hid behind the bushes and waited. Lum, my brother, and the dogs circled and stirred up all the rabbits in the territory.

"Here they come, running like—like scarit rabbits. They run and dived headlong for their old familiar hole in the log. But now, instead of a hole in a safe old log, they knocked themselves senseless and bashed their brains out over my board. The rabbits piled up so fast I had to work hard keeping them carcasses throwed back out of the way. When we finally got through with our rabbit round-up that day, we counted ninety-nine rabbits lying there scattered on the ground around that log with the painted hole. And somebody asks me why I didn't make it one more and come out with an even one hundred dead rabbits. An' I tell them what!? Me tell a lie for one damned ol' rabbit!?

Walking On Water

"I got to studying about this time in the Bible where Jesus walked on the water. Wasn't there some way I could do something like that? Hit would be quite something to show off with in the crowd at Coble's Mill Pond on a Saturday or Sunday afternoon. Boy, I'd be the talk of the whole river settlement. Dishpans on my feet might do it. I studied and experimented. I needed one more dishpan, so I snuck Granny's from the pantry.

"One cold February day we were ready to try it out in a quiet nook at the river ford. Lum helped me. I had my shoes bradded in the center of each dishpan. I practiced walking and lifting the pans some, then I lunged for the water. I made it fifteen or twenty feet all right, but then my feet got too close together and got tangled and tripped me and I fell on my face in the water. With them pans fastened to my feet, I couldn't get up or out and I woulda drowned if Lum hadn't jumped in and pulled me out. Both of us nearly froze to death. I got some gum and wax and tried to seal up the holes in Granny's dishpan. But after a few days it got to leaking and she got suspicious. Then Lum got mad at me and told her whut I done to her pan. She grabbed me and tanned my hide good—plumb wore me out. And that's the last time I ever tried to walk on the water.

Lengthy Barrel

'We traded fer this ol' muzzle-loader rifle with a long barrel. Unusually long barrel. So long it woudn't go inside the house. Had to keep it under the house and in the barn. One day I went squirrel hunting with it and tried to shoot this squirrel out of the top of a high tree. But fer some bloomin' reason I never could hit the varmit. Shot at 'im eight or ten times. Finally Lum comes to see why I'm wastin' so much powder. I tell him I just can't hit the squirrel. That it must be jinxed or something. 'Idgit,' he snorts, 'back up some. Hell, the end of the barrel is four foot tother side of the squirrel!' I did. I backed off down in the holler and took aim and fired and the squirrel tumbled out the first time. After that, ever time I hunted with the gun I had to have somebody to go with me to tell me where the end of the barrel wuz.

Big Corn

"My corn crop that year wuz the finest of the river. I worked hard at it. I fixed the land good and fertilized it heavy. I planted it thick and left it thick in the row. Rains came just right. But we weren't prepared for what happent. The field came right up to one side of the house. In the middle of the night, we heard some popping and cracking and carrying-on and couldn't figure out why. Next morning we went and looked and the young corn had begun shooting out of the ground so fast the shoots had missed the stalk and had jabbed down in the middles and were growing new stalks. It looked like a green wavy sea.

"Long 'bout roasting ear time, we'd go out to gather some ears and 'bout ten or eleven in the morning it'd be so dark out in that field we had to take the lantern to see what we were doing. Pretty nigh smother you. The stalks put on so many big ears and got top heavy, they grew their own props to prop themselves up with. They joined arms at the top to hold themselves together. When we finally got that corn harvested and started feeding it to the mules, they nearly choked each time they tried to eat one of them big ears. They'd slobber and whinney and struggle. I'd have to go out with my hammer and chisel and beat the big ear of corn out of their mouths. Then I learned to take my axe out to the chopping block and quarter them ears up—kinda like splitting stove wood blocks—before feeding it to the mules.

Big Punkins

"Punkins growed big on our farm. One time we had half a dozen pigs get lost and we couldn't find them nowhere. We looked and looked in the woods and fields all around. Nothing. For weeks nothing. Then Granny was in the garden and heard muffled hog grunting coming from summers. She called us and we all went running. Lo and beholden, we found a hole in the side of one of the middle-sized punkins and we stuck our head in and in thar wuz all of them pigs done doubled in size and a-running around slurping up that juicy punkin pith and a eating themselves silly.

Outwitted Crows

"I got tarred of the cussed crows pulling up all my young corn in the spring, but nobody could think up a way to discourage them permanently. In spite of all we could do, they'd sneak in and yank up the sprouts and eat them. Had to plant over the second time. They got all that. Hit made me mad, mad, mad.

"So, I planted over the third time. And it came a rain and got the ground damp. I borred a big old heavy road packer that the road men had left parked close by. And I packed down that field of planted corn good and hard and heavy and firm. When I got through packing, it was so tough and hard I knew them blasted crows wouldn't pull up my corn no more. But they shore tried hard. Next morning I went out to look and the whole field was black as the inside of a chimney at midnight, covered with crows. Hundreds and hundreds of them. They had tried to pull up that young corn and found out they couldn't. It made them so mad that they pulled so hard they pulled their heads plumb off. What didn't pull their head off, broke their fool necks.

Big Taters

"Taters grow big around Rocky River. Once we wuz seining and fishing on a new part of the river and we give out of bait for our trot lines. They sent me up the hill to the nearest farm house with a dollar bill to get the man to sell us a dollar's worth of taters to use for bait and to eat some for ourselves. But you know what? When I tole him whut I wanted, he just spat comtemptly on the ground and sez, 'Naw, go on. I ain't guine to ruin one of my taters just to cut you a little ol' dollar's worth off one corner of it'."

High Barn

"We built barns pretty high back then. I reckon the highest one wuz that 'un off of which I dropped my hammer that time. We wuz puttin' on the roof when I got careless and let my hammer slip off the edge and it fell fast. Just the day before I had put a brand new oak handle in it, too. And you know, that barn wuz so high thet handle had done rotted away before that hammer hit the ground.

"I quit farming the year I made my fortune. Just decided to retire right then. I worked hard all year. But everything wuz against me. Land pore, seed no good, mule died, fertilizer too high to buy. Land dry as the Sir Harry. Then when the rain did come it flooded the fields and the grass took everything. When we finally did get harvested thet fall, I found out I had made just seventy pounds of seed cotton and eleven bushels of corn. So, I just sold out fer cash, banked my proceeds and decided to live off the interest of my money...."

THE BUZZARD MAN

The only way I can introduce you to this colorful Uwharrie character is to let this old man start talking and tell his story his way. He survived all the hard knocks of farm work and he practiced the country way of doing things all his long life. See if you can visualize a rugged eighty-year-old who swears, imbibes a little moonshine, bangs his fists against anything and gets up and stomps an imaginary devil or monster that is creeping too close.

"We wuz walking back from the sawmill along this ol' wagon road when we heard this rustling noise out in the bushes beside the road. Me an' Kemp. Kemp is our neighbor boy. So we moseyed out to see what it wuz. We don't believe in no boogers 'er hain'ts. We like to check things out. Me an' Kemp. Pays to do that. We woulda been scairt to death many times long ago if we hadn't checked it out. Son, you remember that. Check it out. Nothing is hardly ever bad as it 'pears to be. So, check it out first.

"Two big, full grown, black turkey buzzards scrawled around in them bushes. Sick as sick can git. I've seen many a sick buzzard before and since, but never nary a one sick as these two. They were puking and gooking all over the place. This green slimy stuff puffed up outta their mouths. They wuz awking and urking, and flinging their heads and a-flapping around all over them bushes. They couldn't fly. Even if they weren't sick, they couldn't fly. They had puked and gooked this green slimy throw-up stuff all over themselves and each other. Glued their feathers together. Spilled all over their backs and in their eyes. They could hardly move their wings. They had the scrawniest, thinnest necks. Like them necks were just waiting for the axe to fall. If them buzzards had been humans, I do believe they woulda begged somebody with a shotgun to shoot them dead.

"Well, me and Kemp got this idea. Let's keep these buzzards penned up a while, 'til they git over their sick spell, then we can have some big-time BOOMY fun with 'em. I'm sure Kemp knowed what I meant. Kemp's smart. He catches on. But it was the most disgusting, disgraceful thing we ever did, lugging them big birds to a little pen in the edge of the woods near our house. We used the pen to fatten hogs, wean calves, fatten up a possum now and then. But now it was empty and the buzzards would fit in okay. Nasty as it was, we tied some vines around the buzzards' legs, run a sapling through their legs and lugged them on to the pen. We went by the creek and dipped them in the water to try and wash off some of thet scummy stuff, but it didn't do much good.

"We kept 'em penned two-three days and the buzzards felt better and looked better. 'Bout back to their old self. We fed 'em a little corn, a spoiling baked sweet tater and Kemp threw 'em in a dead rabbit once. Kept water to 'em. Just me and Kemp knew about 'em. If Pa had found out about them buzzards he woulda raised a ruckus. Pa gets hot about stuff. When Pa gets mad, he gets mean and when he's mean he tears people up. Never again do I want him mean at me. I ain't got over that last time.

"Then came the day fer our fun BOOMY day.

"Pa and Ma and my brother and sister were going away for the day and leaving me at home to look after everything—feed all the animals, water 'em, milk the cow, gather the chicken eggs, fasten all the gates and doors. They knew Kemp would help me. Ma left enough food cooked for our dinner. They hadn't been gone long when we got them buzzards out and brought them over to the little old log building with a stout door where Pa kept his dynamite locked up in. Here's where we were gonna have our fun. I got the key outta its hiding place and unlocked the door. Inside were several sticks of dynamite, caps and fuses left over from a week ago when Pa and my older brother were dynamiting stumps in the new ground.

"Meantime, we decided to experiment with one buzzard. We didn't need two fer the big BOOM. One would do. So we untied the legs of one, throwed him upwards high as we could and watched him take off. He flapped higher and higher, rose way over the woods and landed on top of a tree where he sat there looking back at us. Okay, we said to the second buzzard, that's exactly what we want you to do—go fly to your friend over there in the treetop.

"Get him fixed," Kemp told me. "Let's git 'im ready to send off.

"We tied two sticks of dynamite together, then tied these to the buzzard's legs and feet. We worked the caps and fuses so both sticks would blow up together. We left the fuse about two feet long. Okay, everything's ready. We lit the fuse and both of us heaved the buzzard into the air over our heads. Because of the extra weight, this buzzard had to flap harder and work harder to gain altitude. But he made it up a ways, then circled around like he didn't know what to do or where to go.

"Then, GAWUD A-MIGHTY, he didn't fly toward the woods, the damn buzzard flew to the barn. I guess' cause it wuz the closest place for him to land.

"He landed right on the peak of the barn roof, right in the middle, right on top of the ridge capping.

"We could see, almost hear, that fuse a-sparkling and a-buzzing and all that buzzard did was look down and try to fig- ure out what was wrong with his landing gear.

"We turned into maniacs. Horrified maniacs. Hysteri- cal, hell-bent maniacs. Blobs of fear as big as oceans burned through our minds. We couldn't let that buzzard stay there. If that dynamite went off there it would blow a hole big as a freight train through that barn roof. Probably set the barn on fire, too, and lose all of it. Pa would kill me.

"We tried everything under the sun to scare that buzzard off the barn roof. We hollared, screamed, shouted, begged, prayed. We threw rocks, corncobs, green apples, sticks, jars. I even throwed my prized Barlow pocket knife at him. He ignored us, still fascinated by the colorful sparks and misty smoke rising from his feet. Kemp found an old rusty tin bucket and beat on it with a stick to drive the buzzard away. But it didn't work, either. I wuz so scared and panicked I wuz about to throw up. Then I wuz ready to give up. Kemp was, too. A horrified picture of a broken, torn and mutilated body–ME–was all my mind could see if Pa came home to a ruined barn. He wouldn't bother Kemp. Kemp was the neighbor boy. But Pa would double up his mean punishing pleasure on me. I had to do something.

"Then it hit me. I knew what I had to do. I'd run away from home.

"Salty tears burned outta my eyes and my throat started choking up. I started sobbing. I couldn't help it. Kemp saw me and he understood. He sorta waved goodbye as he headed for home, knowing I was leaving, too. I turned away and started trotting out the long driveway toward the main road. I'd heard folks talk about Florida. I'd go to Florida. I'd hitchhike. Every time I got a ride, I'd tell them to take me toward Florida as far as they could. Florida was south. I knew which way south was. It was a mighty tender age to be running away from home. But I had to do it. I couldn't face the alternative. Maybe some day when Pa got ol' and disabled and couldn't beat me no more, I could come back.

"There wuz a bend in the driveway ahead. I slowed and twisted my head for one last look at my ol' homeplace, thinking that I would never see it again in this life. Right then in that few seconds something happened to change everything. Yeah, it changed me completely.

"In that one glance over my shoulder I saw the buzzard lift off the barn roof and flap toward the woods. I stopped, out of breath, and looked. He had just got over the woods, about to reach his friend, when KA-BOOM the dynamite exploded and blowed the buzzard and treetops to smithereens. A few limbs crashed down. That booming sound echoed all up and over them hollers and hills.

"White-eyed and jerking, I slumped down against a tree and rested there for an hour. I think that's when I learned to pray and thank God for saving me. He did. He took care of the situation after we done all we could and give up. And that's a lesson I've used all the rest of my life–do all you can first, then ask God to help you the rest of the way.

"Pa never did find out about the buzzards. He never missed the dynamite, either. Or if he did, he didn't say so. He did look at me real hard a few times, but he never did accuse me of anything.

"Just think of that. If that buzzard had been a few seconds longer about lifting off that barn roof–if I had reached that bend in the road without looking back–I woulda been in Florida all the rest of my life and you'd never seen me and you'd never have a story. Whatta you think of that?"

"KA-BOOM," I said.

MIRACLE AT 100 MPH

Ford built cars back in the thirties capable of doing one hundred miles per hour under choice conditions, and Ol' Red's V-8 was the capable-est car that ever dusted the roller coaster backroads in the southwestern part of the Uwharries. They ate up the roads and spewed them out behind. Folks said of Ol' Red and his V-8, "He never let the engine get cool except when he was working on it."

Other travelers were terrified at being on the same road, much less meeting them.

On day while traveling at their customary speed of 100 mph, Ol' Red and his V-8 met God in a split second of time which lasted an eternity. Beneficent fallout from the ensuing miracle has never ceased.

They crested one hilltop ready to soar to the next when, right in front of them on the wrong side of the road, puttered a rattletrap car occupied by two black men and some children. A head-on crash, probably killing all of them, appeared inescapable. On one side loomed a huge oak tree stump, which would bash out their brains. The other side meant a drop-off into some trees and a rock-studded creek. There was no place to go.

"All right, God, You got me into this fix, so You gonna have to git me out, unless you want me to kill myself and them two black men and kids now," Ol' Red blurted. "I know You here in the driver's seat with me, so, quick, what we gonna do?"

"I didn't get you into anything, you arrogant scalawag," God retorted. "What we gonna do is examine this situation and consider it for a while."

"But...Gawd-almighty, God, we got only a secont or less at the most. What can we do in that little bitty time?"

"Take it easy," God said. "You been traveling at top speed too long. You've got to slow down to live. **I've** got plenty of time. Maybe **you** have and maybe **you** don't. We'll see."

Ol' Red got frantic.

"But, God, Sir, I know you're here and like that, but maybe you just don't understand how terrible serious this is. Look. Ol' Lon and Ol' Jim and them kids in that ol' car out there coming meeting me on my side of the road, just twenty feet away and there's less than a secont to go. I got nowhere to go' er nothing to do—except kill 'em or me."

"Don't you question my understanding," God thundered at a cringing Ol' Red, recoiling behind the wheel. "I ought to let you die right now like so many other foolish motorists have done and keep on doing, unknowing, unaware, ignorant of any source of help. You want to die right now, Ol' Red?"

"No, no, I want to live," screeched Ol' Red, tears on his face. "I didn't intend to question your understanding or power, God. I know you're here and you're in control and you'll do with me what you want to. I expect to die because death is staring me right in the face. But I know you can save me if you want to. But I don't know why you'd want to. I've been a mizerable sinner. I've done everything in the book that's mean and ugly and wrong and sinful. And I've never done much for you, except believe in you.

"I do believe in you, God. I've tried to find you. Plowing in that new ground field the other morning I tried to find you. I called for you. I cried for you. I agonized for you.

"Where were you then, God?"

"I was there in that new ground field with you," God said. "I heard you calling and crying. But you didn't need me badly then, Ol' Red. You was just crying to me out of curiosity. You got to sweat some more first, Ol' Red. You got to mean business when you come to me."

"Hell fire, God! Me with one secont to live and you say I don't mean business," Ol' Red exploded. "Well, I do. I'm so desperate. I wanna live, but you've gotta help me. What you want me to do, kill Ol' Lon and Ol' Jim and them kids in that car?"

"Don't you use blasphemy with my name, you spineless weasel," God roared. "I ought to turn you loose and let you kill yourself right now. You've been asking for it for years. But let's consider it some more. Why do you want to kill Ol' Lon and Ol' Jim and those children?"

"It's partly their fault, being on the wrong side of the road. If I slam into them at a hunnered miles an hour, it might knock them out of the way so fast I could keep control of my car. Course, it will probably kill them all. And I don't want to kill them."

"What other alternatives do you see, Ol' Red?"

"Only to kill myself by bashing thet big stump on one side or crashing off on them rocks in the creek on the other side. There's no other way I can see."

"Does Ol' Lon and Ol' Jim know you're fixing to kill them?"

"Yeah. I'm looking right into Ol' Lon's face. He's scared to death. He knows it's too late to do anything. He realizes he's in the fault. But he can't do anything about it, either. His eyes are getting bigger. His face is even turning white. He knows he's looking at death. So does Ol' Jim. The chilluns do, too. They want mercy but they know they'll never get it, because it's too late now."

"In that case, we'll spare them, then," God said. "As long as they're humble, we'll let them live. If they were otherwise, we'd let you kill them."

"Then, that means I have to die, don't it?" Ol' Red asked forlornly.

"How bad do you want to live, Ol' Red?" God asked.

"Bad enough to do whatever you tell me to do, God, 'cause you're the boss. I'll do whatever you say. You got me into this fix, so now you get me out."

"Wait a minute...whoa!" God said. "I ought to let you blast into that stump and go on to hell right now, if that's the way you feel. In fact, I think I will...."

Ol' Red felt something like a huge fist close around his body and squeeze and shake. He felt like he was being pummeled to death the way a cat plays with a mouse. He screamed.

"You little weasel, you little blasphemous ingrate, you rascal," God scolded. "I didn't get you into anything. This crisis is your doing, not mine. How you solve it is your problem, not mine. Right now it looks like you're doing a bad job of it. You got your prayers all said, Ol' Red?"

"Spare me, God," Ol' Red shrieked. "Please spare me. I done it all, I know that. It wasn't you. I been acting a fool all these years and paying you no mind. So you have no reason for saving me now. But please do, God, 'cause I don't wanna die...."

A long heavy moment or two passed while God pondered whether to spare Ol' Red.

Ol' Red tensed like a banjo string, his eyes bulging at the spectre of death so starkly in front of him.

"It's still going to be up to you, Ol' Red," God said. "You're pretty good at handling that steering wheel and that car. So let's see just how good you are. When you touch ground I want you to jerk that wheel hard and warp your car up edgewise and let it skid through up on its side between Ol' Lon's car and that big stump. You ready?"

Ol' Red started to protest that there wasn't room for his car to go through there even edgewise, but he stopped. He gripped his steering wheel and nodded to God that he was ready.

"Now!" God barked.

In a flash of 100-mph action, Ol' Red jerked the wheel as his car touched ground and felt the vehicle lurch on its side and half skid, half fly through the opening, which seemed to widen magically to accommodate him. Later, he learned that even in this edgewise position, his car scraped bark off the stump on one side and paint off Ol' Lon's car on the other. Both Ol' Lon and Ol' Jim were white as ghosts.

"Now," God commanded, "throw the weight of your body upward so the car will flop back on its wheels as you cross the bridge."

Ol' Red did so and the car tilted back on its wheels just in time to skid across the low water bridge, whereupon it slid around and hurtled backwards along the side ditch at 75 mph.

"Boy, I got out of that one slick," Ol' Red chortled.

Immediately an unseen fist slammed him in the chest and tightened. He squalled in pain and fright. God's voice grated in his ear.

"There you go taking all the credit yourself." God warned. "You're not even grateful. Look at Ol' Lon and Ol' Jim. See how grateful they are? They're out of their car and jumping up and down and raising their hands in hallelujah praise to me for delivering them, because they know it's a miracle. But you, you scroundel, you're already gloating about how you'll tell all your cronies how you got out of this tight spot.

"You'll brag about all the heroic stuff you did. You haven't learned your lesson yet, Ol' Red. I can still let that car flip over and kill you deadern' a doornail right now. Maybe I should. You've had your chance. You're hopeless."

As Ol' Red felt death closing in on him again, he screamed and cried out his repentance. He asked God to forgive him and give him another chance.

The car, plowing out the sideditch, gradually lost momentum and stopped amid a cloud of dust. Ol' Red fell out on his knees and kissed the ground and lifted his arms and eyes heavenward in praise and thanksgiving.

"From now on this is Holy ground around here and you remember it," God warned him.

"Yes Sir," Ol' Red said. "Yes Sir."

*   *   *

From that day onward, Ol' Red quit driving and acting like a fool and settled down to some serious study and worship of God, Whom he recommends to everyone all the time, and especially in times of crisis. Many times since that day in the thirties, he talked with God and their relationship solidified into a rapture wonderful to behold.

"I wish everyone could know God and His miraculous power the way I do," Ol' Red testified. "What wonderful changes it would bring in your lives and in the world around us. And it's so easy. He's right at your fingertips. He's eager for you to meet Him. But He expects you to want Him enough to seek Him out. Please don't wait to meet Him like I did, until you rise off a hilltop on a narrow dirt road at a hunnered miles an hour."

THIS OL' HOUSE

Is it possible for an inanimate object like an old house beside the road to frequently change its outward appearance and even to register emotional expressions upon its countenance? All by itself?

After many decades of experience with the historic old DeBerry home on Pee Dee Road in Montgomery County, I am a believer in the affirmative. It remains one of the most expressive inanimate "characters" I have encountered in the Uwharries. And I have been recording colorful characters here since World War II.

This old house caught my attention even earlier, back in my high school days. It has been expressing to me ever since. I average passing this old house several times a year and it's still communicating with me today. This camaraderie will continue as long as both of us survive. I can tell when I'm getting near. My senses perk up. Expectancy takes over. Always I slow down. Often I stop. Soon as I come in sight, the old house surrounds me with warmth and friendliness. Almost, I can feel its arms out-stretched to receive me. It greets me as a welcome passerby or visitor.

Our bond has become so strong through the years, there's no longer any guesswork about what we want from each other.

The old house wants appreciation, companionship of a sort and an outlet for its expression.

I want stories, legends, folklore tales from this area, and if this material involves the old house, so much the better.

Our relationship has been and continues to be mutually satisfactory.

The old house told me about...

...the devil who could be seen at night, sometimes sitting in a window sill, sometimes floating or walking around the upper story of the old house—all the while juggling balls of fire.

His unusual performance was calculated to draw people closer. The closer the better. A few daredevils got brave enough to stand directly under the juggler and watch his actions. Occasionally, the juggling devil dropped a ball of fire toward an individual below. If the individual was brave enough to catch the ball of fire, or attempt to catch it, the fireball quickly extinguished itself and the person was not hurt or burned, nor did he experience any ill effects. Rather, his bravery was intensified and he lived to tell many a wondrous tale about besting the fireball-juggling devil.

However, if the person saw the fireball descending toward him and ran to escape it, it was a different story. He was unworthy. He got branded. The fireball pursued him and seared a painful burn somewhere on his body, marking him as a candidate for the devil's domain.

Plainly, the devil preferred cowards. Exceedingly brave people might find a way to escape his clutches in the hereafter so he gave them more consideration.

The old house told me about...

...the beautiful young bride who could be seen occasionally floating around the premises, day or night, in her lacy white, long-train wedding gown. Everything looked so perfect you could almost hear wedding music and feel the festive atmosphere. Only one thing the startled viewers missed–her head.

Supposedly, the head is hidden somewhere around the house and grounds.

That's what motivates the ghost to come back and look for it. Once reunited with its head, the ghost will no longer appear.

How the bride lost her head is not made abundantly clear and generates much speculation.

One theory is that she was jilted at the wedding. The would-be groom did not show up. He just disappeared and was never heard from again. She suffered maniacal frustration and embarrassment. She ordered the plantation slaves to decapitate her body after she had killed herself and to hide her head where it can never be found. Apparently, the slaves followed through and never told anyone the location.

Another theory says the bride's father was violently opposed to the wedding; that with the help of some of his slaves, he killed the would-be groom and buried his body in a hidden grave on the premises, resulting in another prowling ghost. This male ghost still looks for its bride, but doesn't recognize her without her head.

Long ago, a renowned psychic medium from New York allegedly came to try contacting this ghost and easing it on into the happy haunting grounds. He had little luck.

The only thing remembered was he said the ghost of the bride was trying to contact the ghosts of the slaves who had participated in the killing. If she could make these ghosts show her the location of her lover's grave, then maybe she could contact him and convince him of her identity and they could get back together again.

Then both of them could look for her head.

The old house told me about...

...a related specter.

One temporary occupant of the old house said on several occasions he was approached through a locked door and through the walls by an extremely pretty young woman who had a sardonic smile on her face. Horrified, he emptied his pistol at her figure. But the bullets went right through her body without effect and thudded into the walls. When she got to him, she dissolved around him like a wisp of smoke.

The only variation in her routine was that sometimes she held a glass or goblet in an outstretched hand, as if offering him a drink. What was in the glass? Water, tea, coffee, milk, home-made wine, moonshine? Or poison? Maybe this real-life young woman died of poison. Now, in an effort to retaliate, she offers a poison drink to anyone who will take it. Which accounts for her smile.

Ghost hunters are warned not to accept, at least not to drink from the glass she proffers so invitingly.

The old house, told me about...

...unexplained bobbing lights and savage winds slashing the treetops in the woods around an old slave graveyard on the edge of the grounds. Dozens of slaves are purported to be buried in sunken, unmarked graves here.

This turmoil occurs on quiet nights with no wind stirring anywhere. Nor are there any other lights around which could be mistaken for those at the slave graveyard. Abruptly, a light starts swinging resembling that of a kerosene lantern hanging by its creaky wire handle. There's a crack like a pistol firing into the air. Maybe a rousing shout or two. The ominous snap of a bull-whip brings a painful human whimpering sound. Then the wind acts up, like a whirlwind twisting the bushes and trees just over the graveyard, perhaps an attempt to camouflage the activities below.

Claims are made that the ghosts in this graveyard reenact the realities of 150 years ago and more. The old plantation master appeared before daylight with his lantern, pistol and whip to roust the slaves from their squalid quarters for another long day of hard labor. He tolerated no rebellion or excuses. The pistol and whip were regularly used on laggards. Some say the restless wind is the manifestation of the resentment from the abused slaves, a mysterious occurrence which you can hear to this day.

The old house has told me about...

...a half-grown pig slamming into the floor, as if dropped from above, then squealing and scampering noisily off straight through the walls.

...heavy, but invisible weights tumbling down the stairs.

...wooden shutters, long removed from beside the windows, still banging away in stormy times.

...the distinct sounds of a derelict fiddler still fiddling away up in the attic on a Saturday night.

...the agonizing gasps of a dying person coming from the empty space under a bed.

...a set of false teeth chattering and clattering around the floor as if trying to find the coffin to get into with their owner long deceased.

There are a few more ghosts that the old house didn't tell me about. Live people who experienced them told me.

Decades ago two elderly partners, A. L. Burch and Erwin Stenson, turned the old DeBerry home into the Pheasant Farm, an elite eating establishment known all over the Eastern Seaboard for its customized specialty food, including pheasant. Along with operating the restaurant, they developed another specialty exposing the ghosts they encountered around the old house. This continued for a number of years.

Three examples stand out.

An elderly widow woman once occupied an upstairs room and she operated her spinning wheel all day on Sundays in preparation for making clothes for her grandchildren. This taboo practice of working all day on Sunday was frowned on by the local populace. But she did it, anyway, for years. She died and the room became empty, but the spinning wheel noise could still be heard, especially on blustery days. Local visitors pointed it out to Burch, who heard it many times.

He began systematic investigation.

Upon hearing the noise, he rushed upstairs and traced the noise to the room formerly occupied by the old lady and her spinning wheel. Yes, the noise did resemble that of an operating spinning wheel. But where did it originate? On the first few visits to the room, he was unable to determine the source. Then, one breezy winter day, he inspected the room carefully and found it.

One part of the window casement had rotted away, leaving a vertical opening a couple inches wide. Trapped inside this cavity, a durable splinter rattled and vibrated when the wind blew hard around it. The resulting noise was not unlike that of a spinning wheel in its circular glide. Burch removed the splinter and, thus, waylaid the ghost.

A peg-legged miser lived in the old house for a few years. Each night, he climbed upstairs to count his gold pieces, then back down to his bed, his peg leg making sharp thudding sounds on the wooden stairs. Years after his death, local people claimed you could hear his ghost climbing up and down the stairs at night. Watch the stairs all you wanted to and you'd never see anything unusual. Yet, you could plainly hear the peg leg rapping on the stairs.

Burch pondered for some time before he solved this one.

On a ledge outside the window near the head of the stairs, he found a curl of heavy rusty wire hanging from a nail. When the wind blew, the wire swiveled on the nail, striking one side of the ledge with a "plink" and on the other side with a "plunk." Imagination did the rest.

One inside door in the middle of the old house wouldn't stay closed. You could walk through the door, close it, walk on across the room, turn around and see this door slowly drifting open again. Nearby, an empty rocking chair tended to start rocking a little bit by itself. A bit of engineering ingenuity allayed these ghosts. Burch went under the house and jacked up two sagging old foundation timbers. The door stayed closed. Neither did the rocking chair rock by itself anymore.

I've seen the old house assemble its rough features into a scowl, a frown, a warning glare, almost like a wagging finger ultimatum that you better stay away. It appears to have an element of invincibility surrounding it; like it has the ability to protect itself from vandals and undesirables. On the other hand, it can assume that inviting, almost sexy look, to draw individuals to the premises just to scare the daylights out of them. I've even been a victim of its come-hither look. On the premises once, I heard a cracking, splitting noise and before I could move, a big dead limb fell out of a tree landing just a few feet from me. I was unhurt but scared silly. Just a reminder that the old house is still in control.

Nowadays I don't stop by the old house as much as I used to. It understands. It's always there, patient and abiding. It's up to me. It's never going to reach out and pull me to it. I can tell by the time I come in sight what kind of mood it's in, because it alternates between that inviting look and that stay-away look.

One of these days, I may stop and tell it a story.

THE VOICE

Just like that elusive spot on the highway where your vehicle appears to roll uphill by itself, there's another place in the Uwharrie Mountain vastness where, if you listen long enough, you'll hear a mystic voice offering encouraging words.

Encouraging words tailored just for you and your current situation, no matter what that current situation is.

Various names and references have been assigned to this voice through many generations of folklore.

They call it "the voice".

Also, it's referred to as the counselor, the judge, the advocate, the booster, the deliverer, as well as weightier terms like the intercessor, the savior, the salvationist, the shepherd, the prophet and teacher.

No one can tell if the voice is male or female, young or old, foreign, domestic or otherworldly. Always it is clear and distinct, modulated, authoritative, omniscient. And always customized to the grasp of the recipient.

No personal problem is too big or too small to activate this mysterious voice with its encouraging words—if you find the right location, if you are patient and listen, and if you believe strongly and approach the encounter with expectancy.

McNabb Longshoot claimed he got cheated in a mule trade. Furious, he rampaged about it for days, seeking ways to get even. Finally, he went looking for the voice and found it in the remoteness of the big woods on his extensive farmland. Af-

ter many minutes of meditation, he said the voice spoke to him
out of a tree trunk. It told him to simmer down, to rid himself of
resentment, to go ahead and use the mule he had traded for, the
mule he thought was inferior. The mule turned out to be the best
mule he ever owned and after utilizing it regularly for a year or
two, he sold it for a handsome profit.

Desperation–individuals burdened with problems without solutions–activated the voice more readily.

Never did it appear automatically. Just because you had a
problem did not mean you would be favored by a close encounter with a mystic voice. You had to exert strong effort, exhaustive
effort. Rarely did the voice materialize audibly until the searcher
reached the point of giving up.

Meachus Townsend remembered what his father told
about his grandfather's experience.

"He was down by the river–ol' Rollin' River–ready to
jump in and drown hisself. Then, by cracky, he did jump in,
went plumb under. Maybe had his pockets full of hoss shoes
and plow shovels, I dunno. Anyway, the river wouldn't have
'im. Throwed him back out. His overalls caught on a snag.
Then a big wave came by, a BIG lappin' wave. It got under
him and hoisted him up on the edge, then tossed him like a
driftwood log way upon the bank on dry land. He lay there
swa-gaggin', grovelin' and jerkin', till he got his breath back.
Then, he swore and said, 'I failed at everything else and now,
damnit, I can't even do away with muhself.'

"He was a-mind to jump back in and try again, but the
river stopped 'im. Ol' Rollin' River stopped 'im cold. He said
another big wave came close to the bank and outta' it came a big

muscular arm ending in a knotty oak fist which shook in his face. It splattered drops of water all over him. He got the message plain and clear.

"Then the river calmed down and went back to its normal flow. He sat there leaning his back against a tree trunk. Everything got quiet, still and peaceful. Then the voice started speaking to him.

"It said, 'Meach, you're a lowlife failure because you wanna be that way. You're a coward, a big baby, a whiner and complainer and debunker. All you wanna do is grouse and glower and mutter and ridicule. You open the door to failure and invite it in. Now it's a permanent resident. You keep it well housed and clothed and nourished and won't let it leave.'

"'Meach, why don't you wake up and become a man? Accept responsibility. Find your bootstraps. Mobilize your inner resources. Kick failure out and ban it from your premises forever. Replace it with unending effort, with initiative, imagination, vision, strategy. Recognize and utilize opportunity. Cultivate good friends who'll help you along. Learn to care and share and love everybody. Now get up off your mizzerable rear end, quit your moping and get to work.'

"Pa said grandpap went to work and never stopped. He made his farm so attractive and productive, he sold it and bought two more. Later, sold one of them and bought two more and so on. He lived to be ninety-three and owned a dozen farms, all of them successful. He learned to help people and they helped him back. Grandpap left all his children well off, even his grandchildren. Why, this here land we're on now used to be one of his farms."

Mock Uhree's despondency turned into abject despair after his fiancee broke their engagement and married his rival. He was about to self-destruct when the voice spoke to him one sunshiny day in the hilltop hideaway where he went hoping nature would assuage his misery. The voice didn't condemn or criticize. It merely told him to carry on with his head held high, to be kind and helpful to everyone; then to watch his life improve. Within a year, he was happily married to a wonderful girl from a nearby town.

About the same thing happened to Clare O'Nett when her sweetheart ran off and abandoned her, never to return. In a frenzy, she flung herself off a tall building to bring closure to her consuming grief. On the way down, her tumbling body struck a shrub which cushioned its impact with the ground. Nevertheless, she sustained a broken leg, broken back, concussion, rib and lung damage, and was hospitalized for months. Clare knew about the voice and began pleading for its help. After a few days of silent solicitation, a strange thing happened.

She told about it later to a friend:

"Yes, it was the voice. I know it was. But it didn't talk much. It came in a vision. Not a dream, now, a vision. The voice had personality, a body of sorts. It seemed to take me by the hand and lead me. I wasn't crippled anymore or bedfast. I was walking or floating effortlessly. I saw gorgeous scenery, majestic mountains and valleys, golden palaces and cathedrals, radiant people, angelic singing and music, and I could feel wholesomeness and righteousness everywhere. Love just permeated everything. I felt completely whole and normal. Next day they made tests and x-rays. The discharging doctor smiled and shook his head and said I had made a miraculous recovery. My life has been miraculous ever since. And you know the secret? Helping other people while you help yourself."

Daredevil boys set out to find and expose the voice, but never succeeded.

Country clergy wavered between endorsing the voice for all the good credited to it and condemning it as a cult voice to pull away church members.

Rev. Mayfield McGent, widely known as "Preacher Mac", decided to confront the voice and determine its authenticity. He talked to several people who had experienced the voice and learned all he could about it. He visited these known locations without success. He meditated at remote locations, including his own secluded study. Still no luck. He blustered and ranted and challenged the voice to manifest and debate. Nothing. Puzzled at his inability to arouse the voice, he pondered and analyzed. The answer came, independently from the voice. He had no pressing personal problem bordering on desperation. So he tried another tactic. Intervention. Several members of his congregation were in desperate straits. Could he represent them? Plead in their behalf for the voice to take action? Time after time, he tried, but his best agonized efforts brought no response. Depressed at this failure, his frustration led to dereliction of his church and his eventual dismissal as pastor. Some folks said the voice may have worked for Preacher Mac, but worked the wrong way, since his effectiveness as pastor ended abruptly. He died ignominiously but convinced of the voice's reality.

Other clergymen looked differently at the voice.

Why bother about the validity as long as it was constructively helpful to its select few contacts? Was it of divine origin? Why did desperate pleas to it bring better results than traditional prayers to God? Should church leaders embrace and encourage the voice or ignore it? Continuing testimonies ruled out hoaxes or hallucinations.

Tuff Tombee told how the voice converted him from virtual outlawry to respectability.

"I was mean and tough, a redneck renegade, wouldn't listen to nobody. Done a lot of mean things. Drunk whiskey, even made moonshine, played poker, stole money and property, broke in homes and places, rode about like a wild maniac, broke up marriages, abused women, burned down a house and a barn or two, beat one man almost to death, shot and wounded another, robbed one store, vandalized the church.

"I'd heard about the voice, but didn't really believe in it. I didn't need it. Back then I needed nobody nor nothing. I didn't go looking for the voice. It found me. Up there on that little bluff over the creek, where you can look off and see the town here. That's where I went sometimes to ponder what new meanness I could get into next. That is where it hit me. Hit is right. Like a thunderstorm inside me or a ton of bricks, or an earthquake. Maybe a tornado. I never knew a voice could hurt you or punish you like this. Felt like a hoss whip a-larrupping me or a branding iron a-burning. All inside me.

"When that voice got through chastising me—that's a word the preacher uses—it told me right quick, plain as day, what I had to do if I wanted to keep on living. Quit all my meanness, my rough, tough living, my criminal acts and my deceitful ways.

Start over, made amends. Go to church. Earn a honest living. Help people. I've done it all, too. With tears all over my face, I've been back and apologized to every person I've hurt or wronged. I've paid all my debts and paid for all the property I've stole. I work almost every day and night farming and mechanicing and make a good living. You better believe I help other people, too. I got a group of boys who come out here and I teach 'em all kinds of trades. I tell 'em about the voice and how to listen for it. We don't hear the voice much anymore, but we know it's here watching over us."

Percival Klutz wanted to perceive. He not just wanted to, he became obsessed with a lifetime goal of ferreting out and examining this voice he'd heard about all his life in the Uwharries. One of only a few college graduates of the time, he majored in psychology and education. He taught for three years in the Big City, then came back to the Uwharries where he got a job as a part time teacher and part time store clerk.

Intelligent and gifted with perception and discernment, he spent the majority of his time running down leads on the voice which he fantasized about experiencing himself one day. Tall and bespectacled, Percy looked like the absent-minded professor. Some people avoided him because of his highbrow talk. He knew this would be no obstacle in his eventual communication with the voice because it could adapt to any level.

Systematically, he interviewed every known person who had experienced the voice, prying from them minute detail, description and speculation. Repeatedly, he visited every location where these experiences occurred, spending long meditative hours there, hoping he might be so favored. He began exploring similar locations throughout the Uwharries—scenic hilltops, idyllic streams, remote glens, tranquil old homesites, meadows filled with wild flowers, beckoning old churchyards and cemeteries.

Years passed.

In his ramblings, the aging Percy became an oddball pathetic figure, tolerated sympathetically by the locals, but regarded with suspicion by newcomers and strangers. His eccentricities resulted in weird behavior. Officials were called to escort him off private property and steer him homeward.

Eventually, a new approach developed.

Percy took his evidence and presented it to a group of his college grad contemporaries. After several brainstorming sessions, they reached a unanimous conclusion—it wasn't the location, but the frame of mind that activated the voice. Just a matter of intense concentration. So, test it out. Each contemporary would experiment with this concept in his individual location. Percy would do likewise in the Uwharries. Periodically, they would evaluate their results, if any.

Not much is remembered about Percy, or the voice, after that, although the voice did manifest to a few more deserving people.

Some folks maintain that Percy, even in his advanced age, never quit searching for the voice; that wherever you saw him—walking along the road, in a crowd, sitting on a park bench—his face and his unblinking eyes always were in studious concentration. Whether he was actually experienced the voice before he died generations ago is unknown.

But everybody agrees that he has never quit searching.

LADY IN THE LIBRARY

I first met the Lady in the Library as a third grade student in an old country school devoid of much stimulation except for the personalities involved. She topped the list in this category. She topped most other lists, too, lists of ennobling characteristics. Third grade has been a long, long time ago, but I remember her vividly. She played a pivotal role in my life.

Compared to the other characters profiled in this book, she was a Saint, fully deserving enshrinement in some national monument. In my mind, she's already there, probably in a much better place.

Once a week, our third grade class went to the library for an hour to check out books, flip through magazines, newspapers and the one set of encylopedia. Libraries didn't mean much to me then. Although an average student, I didn't care much for school or studies and I goofed off a lot. Nobody had ever bothered to get me fine-tuned and focused. I was a loose brain wandering randomly.

One day when I stood at the library window watching the winter wind lash the branches of an oak tree, a large adult hand gripped my shirt collar and tugged. "You come with me," her voice commanded. Her hand propelled my shirt collar and me over between two high rows of shelved books. The other hand finger walked across the spines of books. It stopped and pulled out a book. The Lady in the Library bent low her sensitive face up close to my startled one.

"Young man," she said, "here is an excellent book. It's filled with adventure and excitement. I think it was meant just for you. You will love this book. Take it to that table over there and start reading it right now. Take it home with you and read it every night the rest of this week. Then you bring it back and tell me how you like it.'"

I did as she directed. When I opened the pages, something magical happened. That book sprouted arms and pulled me into it—and never let go. That book whirled me into a world of grandeur and wonder like nothing I had ever experienced.

Never in my life have I been more absorbed with a book.

It was about an Indian boy and his family hundreds of years ago—how they discovered and harnessed fire, water power, wind power; how they trapped fish and hunted game animals, foraged wild fruits, grew vegetables, made butter and cheese from milk; how they made tools and weapons, clothing and shelter; how they communicated by smoke signals; how they reckoned time by the moon, stars, sun and seasons, and dozens of other fascinating things.

I could not let go of that book.

It never left my sight, hardly my hands, for the next several days. I read it the rest of that school day, riding home on the school bus, doing my chores around home, at the supper table, around the fireplace. I even took it to bed with me. Saturday, my family went to town for shopping—a special treat in those days—but I stayed home and read the book. Sunday, I concealed it under my sweater and took it to church services, sneaking glances at it while my mother frowned disapproval. By library time the following week, I must have read that book through at least fifteen times.

I sidled up to the Lady in the Library, the book clamped tightly under my arm, and begged her to let me keep it. I broke down and sobbed as she pried the book away from me.

"I love this book," I pleaded. "Let me keep it. I've read it fifteen times. I'll read it again every day. Please, let me keep it, please."

Rarely have I ever seen such joy on a person's face. She glowed. She beamed spiritual energy into me. I could feel it. She hugged me. She was ecstatic because a good book had launched me into orbit as a reader and book lover. Right then and there she had made a book lover out of me. She knew I would never be a problem in school again. She had salvaged me from mediocrity and pointed me toward a higher plane. She had focused me.

She bent down low again, the book between us, her wrinkled face up close to mine. Her gray hair was pulled into a knot behind her head. Her gnarled hands shook a bit gripping the book. She wore spectacles. I could feel and I could see pure radiance coming out of her eyes, along with tears, because she was so happy. Her voice just flowed into me.

"I can't let you keep this book," she said. "It belongs to the school here. We must keep it here for other boys and girls to read and fall in love with as you did. But let me show you something. See those shelves and all those books? You're looking at hundreds of good books, some you'll love just as much as this one. Every library has them. All the rest of your life you can find good books and read them and help other people do the same."

I've done that, too. Through a long career as a journalist and folklorist I've promoted books and the literary arts. But I didn't do enough. Not nearly enough. A little later, I'll tell you how you can help me make up for this glaring deficiency.

In the next few years after that, I read just about every appropriate book in that library, even flipping through the encylopedia pages. Spontaneously, I developed my own system of speed reading and used it to enormous advantage.

It enabled me to read a page faster than most of my contemporaries could read a small paragraph.

I learned all her library procedures and assisted with her work. I knew that library about as well as she did. With the teachers' approval, she entrusted part of her duties to me, as declining health put her on a part-time basis. Practically all library questions, from students and teachers, were referred to me. Whenever anybody wanted a good book to read, she told them to come and ask me, because…"he knows them all."

That Lady in the Library was as proud of me as if I had been her own son.

Then high school came along and the years passed swiftly. No longer did I work in the library, although I patronized it more than anyone. I recommended books and could answer almost any question about them.

Along then is when I drifted into a new dimension in books.

Throughout high school, we had to give book reports, oral or written, about once a month. Most students hated book reports, but I excelled at them. I could deliver oral reports, but I much preferred written ones. Since I had already read most of the books in the library, I got bored working with the mundane ones. Eventually, this boredom led me to a new and very challenging type of book reporting, so esoteric, in fact, that I've never told anyone about it till now, for obvious reasons.

I began making up fictitious book reports. Entirely fictitious. Every word. I invented the title, author, publisher, main characters, did a one-page synopsis and told what I liked and disliked about the book, along with suggestions for improvement. I did this all through high school, earning consistently high grades on each and every report. Not once did any teacher ever become suspicious, question me or call me on the carpet.

The ease with which this was accomplished led to still another expansion of book reporting proclivity.

Other students were aware of how easy book reports flowed through me.

They knew I devoured books. Wherever they saw me, seated or mobile, I had stacks of books around me, or armfuls, more bulging out of my clothing, probably another one opened at arm's length to read as I walked.

So they wanted me to help them do book reports to turn in as their own. I agreed to do so, since all through school I had been encouraged to help other students all I could. So in addition to my own fictitious book report, I would do several more customized ones each month, tailored to the individual student's reading level and articulateness.

One boy gave me a dime for a fictitious book report. A girl gave me a big orange. Another boy let me keep his bicycle and ride it for a whole weekend.

Another boy brought me a baby squirrel, its eyes just opening. I had a good thing going there for a while.

Nobody ever told on me. Nobody could have told on me. Nobody else knew what I was doing. Just me. The students that I did book reports for didn't know the reports were fictitious. They wouldn't have cared, anyway, as long as they received good grades, which they always did.

Looking back now, I wonder about the ethics involved.

Sure, there was deception. But outright, deliberate fraud? I dunno. I created fictitious book reports when they should have been genuine. But I did not feel like I did anything wrong or criminal. Maybe it was a form of cheating. My justification was that I was helping my fellow students as I had been encouraged to do. There was no rule that book reports had to be made from books in the school library.

So, am I guilty of wholesale fraud? Do I have a criminal past? In no way am I bragging about getting away with a serious infraction of school policy, though at the time I was totally un-aware of any such policy, if any existed. I had no criminal intent. All I did was yield to a natural inclination. It was just another outlet for my preoccupation with books—inspired by that dear Lady in the Library.

Even yet, I get troublesome feelings about this. If the school authorities find out about this deception, will they come and try to take my high school diploma away from me? Or in-validate it? Please don't let them do so. I value my high school diploma, it being the highest point I reached along the formal academic road. If such a movement materializes, I hope you will help me fight it.

But back to that deficiency–the part I **didn't** do–the omission that still troubles my conscience. It's a mistake you can help me rectify.

Those years fled by so swiftly and I got caught up in such a welter of activity that I failed to notice as that Lady in the Library grew older, sicker and stopped coming to school. Before I became mature enough to realize what a debt I owed her–that I ought to go thank her most sincerely–it was too late. She had died. Even yet, I have a tinge of heartbreak when I think about it. So, I need your help in rectifying my mistake.

Regardless of your age or circumstances, you can help me whenever you frequent a library, be it private, public or institutional. Each library usually has a friendly lady ready to help you. Make her your personal Lady in the Library. Thank her as often as you can. It will make me feel better.

If you keep thanking her, you may share the same feeling I have. Of all the individuals who boosted me along the way, the most indelible always will be my dear Lady in the Library.

And every time you help me say "thank you", I hope she's somewhere up there listening.

OL' TOBE'S TOMFOOLERY

The most captivating non-human colorful character I ever met in the Uwharries proved to be a pony. A pony of unrivaled uniqueness. If humanity occasionally produces an inimitable rugged individualist, I'm sure the animal world does likewise. Animality almost outdid itself when it produced Ol' Tobe for he tried hard to fit in with humans.

An elderly friend of mine from a distant city stopped off for an overnight visit with us on his way to his college reunion in a nearby town. Freddie and I fixed a portable chair for him to sit in the shade of the old pear tree while we finished some pressing gardening chores in the mild late afternoon. He insisted we bring out a copy of my ghost story book so he could finish some of the stories he'd never read. Soon he was absorbed in his reading and oblivious to everything else.

Occasionally I glanced at him just to be sure he was doing all right. On one such glance, I glimpsed a dim shape materializing far in the background and realized what could possibly happen, but then I dismissed it from my mind as being too remote.

Later a yell shattered the stillness.

"Hey, whadda you think you're doing!"

I knew the remote had happened as I straightened to look.

My tottering old friend had jumped to one side, overturning his chair, dislodging his eyeglasses and dropping his book.

He glared at a dark brown pony standing there admiring him. I ran up to be sure nobody was hurt.

A city man unaccustomed to country critters, he glared indignantly at his new admirer.

"I was sitting here minding my own business when he sneaked up and scared the daylights outta me. Here I was all alone and defenseless, absorbed in one of your ghost stories, all tense and nervous, quite unsuspecting of any trouble. All of a sudden this character pokes a big head over my shoulder and plays cheeky with me. His whiskers jabbed me like needles. His nose was wet and drippy. He snorted right in my ear. I thought a ghost had me and was taking me off to his lair. I couldn't help yelling. He didn't seem to mind me yelling. If he wants this spot, he can have it and I'll move somewhere else. But not the book. Damned if I'll give him this book. If he wants to read your book, you'll have to get him another copy."

Ol' Tobe had found another victim.

I remember quite well the first time Tobe had victimized me.

Tired from hours of typing, I walked out the back door of my rural home, stretched and stood breathing deeply of the chill night air, relaxing as I contemplated the starry heavens. Abruptly, something shoved me from behind and I hurtled forward, almost airborne, until my feet tangled and I sprawled on the ground completely unnerved and groveling in shock. I couldn't help yelling. The suddenness of the attack left me gibbering. As I came to my senses, I saw a faint shape, heard muted hoofbeats and an unmistakable sarcastic whicker. And then I knew.

Ol' Tobe had found another victim! And I was just the latest of many.

Tobe was an oddball dark brown pony we acquired for our six-year-old son, Freddie, hoping to interest him in horsemanship. The seller delivered him in a cattle trailer towed behind a pickup truck.

"His name's Toby," he told us. "He's gentle. I used him to plow my vegetable garden. The kids ride him and play with him. You'll love Toby."

Freddie and I decided his name was one syllable too long so we shortened Toby to Tobe. An average-sized pony, slightly swaybacked and with unshod hooves, Ol' Tobe had a luxurious mane, alert ears, sensitive eyes and whiskers which pointed out at odd angles around his nostrils. He didn't object to us patting and rubbing him or getting his bridle off and on. We could lean against him and let him eat out of our hand. Tobe would go wallow in the dust, then come and shake off the dirt right in our faces like a wet dog shaking off water on your legs. He bared his teeth and whinnied about the same way a dog uses his tail.

But one thing we learned rather quickly—Ol' Tobe didn't go in much for riding or working or anything else requiring strenuous effort.

Freddie never did ride Ol' Tobe but a time or two. Horseback riding, or pony riding, just did not interest him; it wasn't his cup of tea. We didn't insist. Other people rode Ol' Tobe—the people who kept horses in our barn, neighbors, visitors—and he cooperated, once over his inertia. But Freddie just never cared for riding.

I well learned the lesson of an exercise in futility in trying to work Ol' Tobe pulling the plow in my vegetable garden. Controlling the plow and controlling Tobe with the lines at the same time proved much too difficult for one person. Always Tobe would foul up some way, deliberately I'm sure, causing me to lose patience and curtail the work. Ol' Tobe knew he had us buffaloed and he whinnied in sarcastic delight as we took him back to the barn.

From the start, Tobe acted like he was a member of our family. Gradually we allowed him complete freedom to roam the premises at will, which brought into play the full extent of his eccentricities.

Several times after that first shove, he got me the same way. It's difficult to see a dark pony on a dark night, especially if you're absorbed with enjoying Mother Nature as I always was. Silently Tobe sneaked up behind, put his nose down below the seat of my pants, then pushed outward and upward for all he was worth, almost catapulting me into orbit. You have absolutely no defense against such an attack. All you do is hope you land in a soft place. Each time, I cussed, shook my fist and vowed to sell him to the rendering plant. All I ever heard from him was that mocking whinny of laughter.

One summer night, Freddie and I were sleeping outside to watch a meteor shower. In the wee hours, I felt something moist and clammy against my head, and a tugging at my ear. I became aware of a large dark shape bending over me, a hissing, blowing and gurgling in my face. Was Scotland's Lock Ness Monster trying to eat me? Then, I recognized Ol' Tobe. He actually nuzzled and nibbled at my ear, clamped his thick lips over

it and pulled until my ear slipped out of his mouth with a grue-
some pop. I swung at him with my fist as he wheeled away and
whinnied.

On a hot Sunday afternoon in September I was
three-fourths asleep on the lounge chair under the backyard pear
tree when a weird sensation roused me. My head started hurt-
ing, then throbbing. I felt a tough, slurpy object slide across my
forehead. Finally I got one eye open. Ol' Tobe's teeth were
bared, his lips quivered, his tongue lolled out. He licked me
again across the face and forehead before I could resist. I
jumped up sputtering. Had that blasted pony bitten me on the
head?

I touched my throbbing temple and felt something sticky
and oozy. Good Lord, I'll shoot that maniac right now, I
shrieked to myself. Wonder if he was rabid? Almost reeling with
pain, I had actually started to the house to get my shotgun when I
spotted a large ripe pear with a big mushy spot on it lying in the
grass. Then I knew what had happened. From twenty feet up in
the tree, that pear had turned loose, whacked me on the temple
and showered me with pulp. Tobe, being nearby, started licking
the pear pulp off my face.

After dark one summer evening, a carload of visitors
drove up in our backyard. With no outside light on, all was black
except faint light from the house. I had started through the
house to greet the visitors when a commotion startled me.

A kid squalled in terror.

"Hey, what's that?!" screeched an adult.

Doors slammed. More squeals and shrieks. Two adults
and three kids slammed into and through the door simulta-

neously and stood there gasping. All were asking what it was. Slowly, I got the story piecemeal.

When their car stopped in the backyard, there was a slight delay in getting out. An ominous shape thrust through the open window of the passenger door and snorted and shook in their faces.

"I thought it was Big Foot or one of your ghosts out here," the woman said. "Just after the car stopped, this big head poked in the car window right in our faces. It snorted, kinda hissed, then shook itself. Then kinda giggled or squealed at us. Then it vanished. It didn't hurt us, but it sure scared us to pieces."

Several visitors arriving at night were shaken up similarly. In addition to the darkness, Tobe had two excellent places to hide, behind the smokehouse and the well house, near where all vehicles parked. If the car windows were closed, Tobe used another tactic. He'd ease up near the passenger side and wait until the door opened and the people got out. By the time the people closed the door and turned around they were nuzzling Tobe nose-to-nose. This, along with his abrupt snort, his bristly whiskers, his foul breath and his triumphant whinny threw some of the visitors into hysterics. Tobe added a dramatic flourish by rearing up on his hind legs, pawing the air ferociously, then wheeling and galloping off.

Tobe crashed picnics. He participated in practically all our outside activities. He often met the mailman, retrieved our daily paper, served as our official greeter and watchdog. Once he walked up on our waist-high front porch and flabbergasted some important visitors. He mimicked laughter from any source. He'd stand and fuss back at a scolding Blue Jay. We often thought Tobe tried to talk.

Some of Tobe's victims could not understand why we didn't keep him confined and end his mischief. It seemed morally wrong to deny him access to people. The pony loved people. He never harmed anyone. Scared plenty of people silly, but he wasn't vicious. In human terms we'd call him a weirdo or neurotic. His specialty was scaring people and he took perverse delight in it, his instinct and timing perfect. I know because I was his victim more than any other person.

Freddie and I appreciated his whacko personality, but my wife said he was scaring off too many visitors; he was tearing up her flowers and pulling drying clothes off the line.

Dismayed at his new rascality, we ran a classified ad and sold Tobe and all his accessories for $50. The man who bought him asked me if Tobe was gentle and trustworthy. I nodded. I had opened my mouth to tell him about Tobe's idiosyncrasies when something stopped me cold.

A strange premonition gripped me. Telepathy tugged at my mind. I looked at Ol' Tobe. He was eyeballing me hard. The message I got was to mind my own business.

Later I realized that Ol' Tobe had finally talked—his way.

THE STRANGE INTERLUDE

Maybe I dreamed it, maybe I didn't; I guess I'll never be sure which.

But I remember it.

I remember getting out of my car at this nondescript little house on the Uwharrie Mountain backroads. The ancient weatherboarding clung desperately to the sides of the shack and the tin roof glared back squint-eyed at the sun. The steps swayed under my feet and the ragged-edged porch looked hazardous. Out of the dirty front door hung a dejected doorknob, tarnished and twisted after hanging there for decades.

It's a funny feeling when you stand on the brink of something, you know not what.

My body was taunt with anticipation and my mind buzzed with wonder and apprehension. You hear about a thing and you come to find out for yourself if it's on the level. If it is...

Four times I rapped on the rough front door. As I waited a window rattled somewhere back inside the house and the wind whipped powder-fine dust from the yard up around the porch. The dust seemed to settle around my head and I tore loose in a fit of coughing. When I took my handkerchief from my smarting eyes and nose, a wrinkled old woman stood in the doorway looking at me. Her hair was black and straight, her skin a light mulatto, her face blunt and blocky. A woman as plain as this old house by the side of the road.

"It'll take you back," I said, repeating the words that were supposed to be appropriate for this encounter.

Her sharp eyes flicked over me briefly. Then she stepped aside and nodded her head toward the interior of the room. I stepped across the threshold and into the gloom of the room.

That step across the threshold was the last conscious step I remember taking then, although I kept moving...like walking blindly into a black night.

My next impression was like standing on a hill on a windy day and feeling the wind tangling your hair and scrubbing your face. Except this was a sort of thick, heavy, velvety rush of air that you could almost sift through your fingers. I felt it creeping warmly over my body, under my clothes, in my ears, mouth, and through my body. Like a hot mud bath that leaves you clean, relaxed, and refreshed.

Then I was out of the air flow and in a pool of gloom too deep for perception. More like walking through a wall of absolute darkness. At first, I thought maybe I was asleep and dream-drifting but I pinched myself and slapped my face and yelled into the blackness. That yell was a mistake. It brought thunderheads of deafening echoes reverberating around my head and for a minute I thought I would black out into nothingness. But the noise faded and was replaced by a ghoulish symphony sound coming very faintly from somewhere. I know you can't smell music, but for a second or two there I had the crazy notion I was smelling that medley of sound and enjoying it more by nostril than by ear.

Up to this point my eyes had been quite useless in the impenetrable gloom, but now they were attracted to a bright alcove appearing on the right. To my overwhelming astonishment, I came abreast of a strange ivory face outlined against a golden backdrop. It began talking to me. Rather communicating with me, for there weren't any oral words spoken. It said something like, "Greetings," then, "Proceed." Evidently he was just a doorman or flunky around the joint. Several other similar flunkies gave the impression of nodding for me to continue as I passed by.

Next I met Dalmute. Quite a chap he turned out to be. Ramrod of the place. The boss. The super supervisor. He had this same ivory-on-gold countenance and he could talk. His voice was velvety wine gurgling out of a bottle. A plain talker, this Dalmute.

"The ivory and gold stuff on our face is just a facade," he said. "A mask we hide behind. Otherwise you might recognize some of us—now or later—and that would be unwise. You will not get close enough to recognize anyone else. My voice, too, is disguised. The woman you met at the door you will not remember, either."

We were walking, moving, rather, again now into the pitch blackness and ahead of us and off to the left at a lower level; faint patches of light began to appear. And there was movement within those patches.

"But those faces behind us," I said, "and that curtain of warm air that blew all over me?" My voice sounded unnaturally soft and sonorous, blending with the atmosphere of this eerie place.

"An understandable inquiry," Dalmute said. "The warm air, as you call it, purified you both externally and internally and conditioned you in other ways. It sharpens and deepens the latent and acquired abilities and capacities of everyone who passes through, depending upon their natural endowment.

"The other associates along the way are doormen and gatekeepers, you might say. They make lightning appraisals and evaluations of your mentality as you pass. Infallibly accurate, too, I might say. One takes your general intellect, another your emotional responsiveness, another measures your physiological makeup and your sensitivities and reflexes and special aptitudes, and so on. By the time the subject emerges to the point where you met me, we have a thorough digest and analysis of his capabilities. As you shall see, we're interested primarily in any underdeveloped, constructive and potential high-level capacities he possesses which can be cultivated."

We moved along what appeared to be a sort of observation walkway. Below us in a variety of surrounding, people were busy. The illumination was sufficient to see them as human beings, men and women, but not good enough to see their features clearly. I got the impression some were as young as the teens while others were quite aged. Each individual, or pair, or team, occupied a little world of his own.

"Observe them all you wish," Dalmute purred in my ear. "Proceed as far as you like. You can't get any closer or see any better and trying to communicate with them will be useless. I'll rejoin you later."

And he was gone like a light snapped off and I was left alone in this vast strangeness so weird and fantastic I felt my knees trembling and my senses reeling. But calmness and control returned, and with them an invigorating feeling of physical and mental well-being as well as security and eagerness.

These people were unaware that I saw them. They were absorbed in their work and appeared motivated by a passionate devotion and drive. There were no supervisors or instructors or guides or mentors. Each person seemed aware only of the task before him.

Some worked in laboratories and machine shops and at blueprint boards. Some were engaged in what looked like complex experiments involving assorted machinery and equipment. Some sat studying amid shelves of books and papers. Others tapped energetically at typewriters, practiced at the piano, sawed at a violin, made speeches from behind a rostrum, painted at an easel, sang at a mike, counseled at a desk, and performed upon the stages and in the operating rooms.

One man and a magnifying glass hunted insects around the base of a tree in a meadow. A young woman collected botanical specimens in a swamp. A diver explored the bottom of the ocean. Flyers and balloonists experimented at great altitudes. Actors performed in the floodlight and teachers lectured to eager classes. Arbitrators bargained at the meeting tables and hurricane hunters tossed as they took readings in the eye of the storm. Nurses ministered to patients. Preachers condemned and inspired. A robed judge rubbed his chin thoughtfully on his bench. The governmental executive listened attentively in the policy-making session. One man walked around shaking hands and smiling at everyone.

I was boiling with questions by the time Dalmute rejoined me, his stolid face comical in contrast to the gloom.

"But who are they? What are they doing? Where did they come from? What's the point of all this? How do you do it?"

"These people are here because they want to be here and deserve to be here," Dalmute said. "Because they have vital work to do and contributions to make and no time for it on earth. We give them time here, all the time they need, and in whatever setting required and in complete absorption with their project. They have absolute freedom from want and are effectively insulated against all distraction. When their work reaches maturity, they go back into civilization where it may be fruitful."

More questions rose within me. "But their homes, their jobs, their families—how can they abandon all their responsibilities?"

"They don't," Dalmute said. "The time they spend here is entirely separate and extra and doesn't detract one minute from their normal lives at home. Some of them work here full-time more than two years and never miss a minute of their regular earthly domestic routine of home-family-job."

My senses rebelled and I found myself staggered again at the impact and meaning of his words which I did not want to believe, yet which I felt I must accept.

"You mean that these people lead two different lives in two different places at the same time?" My voice was shrill with overtaxed incredulity. "It couldn't be."

"Essentially, that is correct," Dalmute said. "Let's say your views—and perhaps your knowledge, too—on the subject is a bit old fashioned and outdated."

"But don't their two lives get confused?' I gasped. "Don't they remember and wonder and become psychotic?"

"They retain only the increased knowledge and proficiency gained here," he said. "Not even their associations in teams or groups are remembered. Everything is orderly."

"How are they selected for this—this extra life?" I asked him.

"To avoid specifics and to simplify things, let's just say we have something like an omnipresent, automatic system which infallibly selects our candidates. People chosen are those who have faith and belief in themselves, that have drive and initiative and who are eager to work to realize their aspirations. Since our system of selection is perfect and perpetual, there's no conscious thing anyone can do to win acceptance here."

Dalmute added: "You're an observer this time. Our first, as a matter of fact. Perhaps you'll be back sometime as a regular customer, who knows? You might be surprised at some of the great men and geniuses of your world who have sojourned with us.

"You came to us in a roundabout way for a purpose. Rather somewhat of a test.

"When you get back out, you'll find you haven't missed a moment of your normal life. Also, that you will never be able to contact us again in the same manner."

He was silent for a moment as if debating whether his should speak the next words.

"We have another division here, too," he said. "It's re-served exclusively for those hard-working, long-suffering people who never have a chance to take a vacation or rest, recuperate, and re-charge themselves while maintaining their regular pace at home. That way no one loses and everybody gains. It's the only way some of those indefatigable people can keep going. Again, the choice is not theirs to make. We do it."

The next thing I remember I was standing on the porch of that dilapidated house and walking down the steps with my eyes still smarting from the dust. It had been five minutes before 2 p.m. when I arrived at the house and entered. I looked at my watch and it was still five minutes before two and the watch was running normally.

I got in my car and drove to Albemarle, and it seemed like I woke up and came into full consciousness about the time I got into the center of town. I have never been able to remember from which direction I came. Nor have I been able to find that old house out on the Uwharrie backroad from whence I embarked on this most fantastic experience of all.

Fragments of Dalmute's conversation stick in my memory..."They're here because they deserve to be here...contributions to make...does not detract a moment from their normal lives...there's nothing they can do consciously to win acceptance here...idleness is the thing we hate most...just call it an interlude in their lives."

A strange interlude, indeed.

FIFTY DOLLARS

My Uwharrie Muse is an indispensable "character" which grabbed me early and, thank goodness, shows no sign of letting go after all these decades. Our relationship keeps intensifying. Though I cannot see this Muse, I can sense it and feel it instantaneously. Our camaraderie is precious. It gives me guidance, inspiration, extraordinary clarity on my mental screen and it steers me through many an obstacle. I could not perform without it. Following is one of the earliest examples of my collaboration with this "character" from Uwharrie Musedom.

If I had fifty dollars, I'd be as hard to hold, as a pack of pampered puppies, or a racer primed to roll. Fences wouldn't hold me, walls they'd have to go, roads would burn behind me, away, away I'd go. Exotic places would beckon, the country, the cities, the seas, the hills, the mountains, the forests, the sunset, the dawn and the breeze. I'd savor the mist o'er the mountains, the lure of the quaint country, the call of space and openness, and the glitter of urbanity.

Unbridled, footloose, and so eager, no purpose, no reason, no goal, just drifting with fancy guiding, toward the future, the current, and the old. On foot, by 'cycle, by horseback, by rickshaw, train and canoe, I'd glide o'er the earth's wide surface, the rain and wind I'd pursue. No thought of tomorrow or next day, each day I'd live with a song, caressed on all sides by nature, a continuous thrill to prolong.

In Paris, I'd tackle the Eiffel, the beauteous dolls I'd adore, the shops, the markets, the windows, the intrigue and glitter and glamour. In the Orient I'd study Confucius, with sticks eat many a strange dish, learn a hundred and one quaint customs, find out how to love and cherish. In Switzerland, the Matterhorn would call me; I'd visit a watchmaker, too, their cheese I'd just have to sample, and get in on a party or two.

Mountains, I'd cross over, the Himalayas I'd just have to see; in Tibet I'd find those mystic lands where youth has a permanency. All Europe and Asia I'd cover, with the kids trading jackknives and beads, and go with a song and a whistle, to fraternize next with the Swedes. The Channel I'd cross without swimming, no record-seeking for me, then into the fog of great London, to taste its austerity.

I might linger awhile in old England, go fox-hunting with Dukes and Lords, examine old castles and dungeons, see knights with their armor and swords. Palaces and Royalty would enchant me, I'd dine in splendor and pomp, Parliament in session would thrill me, o'er stone walls and brown fields I'd tromp. Its literature I'd avidly devour, smell the fog which serves as its wrap, talk endlessly with all kinds of people, learn to say "bloody", "bully", and "old chap".

Scotland would be next to attract me, the Highlands that Burns has described; there I'd relax in rustic enchantment, a pleasure that can't be proscribed. Its people, its customs, its scenery, would be so endearing to me, I believe I could stay there forever, without any nostalgic reverie. A rosy-cheeked lass I'd endeavor to find, with the twinkle of love in her eye, a Highland cabin in some little cove, and let the rest of the world go by.

A thousand years hasn't changed it, the people and soil are the same, through eternity I'd like to go on looking, calling each hamlet and stream by name. Oh, if the people and the country there, with its music, manners and fun, were wrapped up in a tight little bundle, to be looked at while off on the run. But the call of the wanderer pervades me, up, on and away is the cry, with tears and deep reluctance, I'd bid bonnie old Scotland goodbye.

Ireland, I'm sure would do much to dispel, the heartbreak that leaving had been, 'cause O'Brien, O'Malley, and O'Grady, too, would each have a story to spin. Rare jokes with themselves at the butt, the Irishmen would level at me, gloom couldn't last, mirth would return, and I'd join in their joviality. Deep lagoons in lazy places, dusk and flickering fireflies, mingled with spirited laughter, and soft, sweet lullabies.

At the Irish Sea, I'd sit down and dream, of the Afton the Rye and the Brae, and prior to parting I might slip down and see, the moon over Galway bay. I hope Ireland's spell would release me, ere I became too attached to the land, for twinkles in the eyes of Irelanders, magnetize like a magic band. Its quaintness, its rhythm, its people, sounding like a rapt golden chord, will haunt me in memory forever, like no artificiality can afford.

Restive feet would take me onward, the nomadic instinct I'd obey, the seas no doubt would attract me, I'd sail to the sunset in a dray. High seas would scourge me and toss me, the waves would buffet and churn, currents would drift and guide me, hot tropical suns would burn. Whatever island I beached on, I'd stand up stretch and shout, "I've come to explore and to conquer," with a crumb and cudgel start out.

I'd board a cruiser in Havana, and sail through the South Sea Isles, my adventurer's blood still tingling, to stop where fortune beguiles. I'd tread deep Amazon jungles, cross sweltering plains of Peru, climb frozen Chilean mountains, searching vainly for something new. When the continent could no longer contain me, I'd set sail for Australia and New, cruise back by Antarctic regions, dodge icebergs bobbing along the blue.

To the darkness and mystery of Africa, like a moth to the light I'd go, and even if it took me a lifetime, speaking of Africa I could say "I know". Trails of the Congo would be my backdoor, I'd know every peak in a cloud, I'd learn to beat the natives' drum, and imitate the hippo real loud. Every flower, and animal, every sound and stream, every thing in the exotic land, I'd wrap up in ones and twos and threes, and hold in the palm of my hand.

But such a life would not be conducive, to roots and accumulative frills, but nowhere for entertainment value, could you find such abundance of thrills. A romanticist is about through talking, he's tough when it comes to just talk, but write him a check for a certain amount, and see if his ego don't balk. I won't be leaving tomorrow or next week, or even a month from today, 'cause I ain't got fifty free dollars, to get me the first leg of the way.

Fred T. Morgan is a longtime resident of the Uwharries. He worked for thirty-four years as the award-winning Feature Editor for the *Stanly News and Press*. He has also written special projects for corporations such as Ford and Alcoa, and authored numerous magazine articles. His other books include *Ghost Tales of the Uwharries, Uwharrie Magic, Haunted Uwharries, Uwharries, If These Graves Could Speak,* and *The Revolt and 28 More Original Uwharrie Ghost Stories*. His fascination with the Uwharries began in high school when he learned that they are remnants of the oldest mountain range on the North American continent. Since then, he has explored most of the rural areas in this seven-county area and talked to many of the residents. This is his last book in the Uwharrie series.